Richmond Shall Not Be Given Up

THE SEVEN DAYS' BATTLES
JUNE 25-JULY 1, 1862

by Doug Crenshaw

EMERGING CIVIL WAR SERIES

Chris Mackowski, series editor
Kristopher D. White, chief historian

The Emerging Civil War Series offers compelling, easy-to-read overviews of some of the Civil War's most important battles and issues.

Recipient of the Army Historical Foundation's Lieutenant General Richard G. Trefry Award for contributions to the literature on the history of the U.S. Army

Other titles in the Emerging Civil War Series include

Hurricane from the Heavens: The Battle of Cold Harbor, May 26-June 5, 1864
    by Daniel T. Davis and Phillip S. Greenwalt

The Last Days of Stonewall Jackson: The Mortal Wounding of the Confederacy's Greatest Icon
    by Chris Mackowski and Kristopher D. White

No Turning Back: A Guide to the 1864 Overland Campaign
    by Robert M. Dunkerly, Donald C. Pfanz, and David R. Ruth

Simply Murder: The Battle of Fredericksburg, December 13, 1862
    by Chris Mackowski and Kristopher D. White

That Field of Blood: The Battle of Antietam, September 17, 1862
    by Daniel Vermilya

That Furious Struggle: Chancellorsville and the High Tide of the Confederacy, May 1-4, 1863
    by Chris Mackowski and Kristopher D. White

For a complete list of titles in the Emerging Civil War Series, visit www.emergingcivilwar.com.

Richmond Shall Not Be Given Up

THE SEVEN DAYS' BATTLES
JUNE 25-JULY 1, 1862

by Doug Crenshaw

EMERGING CIVIL WAR SERIES

SB

Savas Beatie

California

First edition, first printing

ISBN-13 (paperback): 978-1-61121-355-3
ISBN-13 (ebook): 978-1-61121-356-0

Library of Congress Cataloging-in-Publication Data

Names: Crenshaw, Douglas, author.
Title: Richmond shall not be given up : the Seven Days' Battles,
June 25-July 1, 1862 / by Doug Crenshaw.
Description: First edition. | El Dorado Hills, California : Savas
Beatie, 2017. | Series: Emerging Civil War series
Identifiers: LCCN 2017011488| ISBN 9781611213553 (pbk) |
ISBN 9781611213560 (ebk.)
Subjects: LCSH: Seven Days' Battles, Va., 1862.
Classification: LCC E473.68 .C743 2017 | DDC 973.7/32--
dc23 LC record available at https://lccn.loc.gov/2017011488

Published by
Savas Beatie LLC
989 Governor Drive, Suite 102
El Dorado Hills, California 95762
Phone: 916-941-6896
Email: sales@savasbeatie.com
Web: www.savasbeatie.com

Savas Beatie titles are available at special discounts for bulk purchases
in the United States by corporations, institutions, and other
organizations. For more details, please contact Special Sales, P.O. Box
4527, El Dorado Hills, CA 95762, or you may e-mail us at sales@
savasbeatie.com, or visit our website at www.savasbeatie.com for
additional information.

This book is dedicated to my very patient and wonderful wife, Judy.

Table of Contents

ACKNOWLEDGMENTS   IX

TOURING THE BATTLEFIELD   XI

FOREWORD   XIII

PROLOGUE   XXI

CHAPTER ONE: Prelude to the Seven Days   1

CHAPTER TWO: Lee Takes Command   9

CHAPTER THREE: McClellan Stirs   19

CHAPTER FOUR: A Creek in Mechanicsville   25

CHAPTER FIVE: Gaines's Mill: The First Phase   37

CHAPTER SIX: Lee's First Victory   51

CHAPTER SEVEN: Savage's Station   65

CHAPTER EIGHT: The Race is On   73

CHAPTER NINE: Down by the River   79

CHAPTER TEN: White Oak: Where is Jackson?   85

CHAPTER ELEVEN: Glendale (Frayser's Farm)   91

CHAPTER TWELVE: The Federal Retreat   105

CHAPTER THIRTEEN: Hurricane on the Hill   115

CHAPTER FOURTEEN: Dawn of the Army of Northern Virginia   123

APPENDIX A: Eyes on the Peninsula: Stuart's Ride around McClellan   133

APPENDIX B: The Civilians   141

APPENDIX C: Preservation Efforts   147

ORDER OF BATTLE   154

SUGGESTED READING   165

ABOUT THE AUTHOR   168

$List$ of $Maps$

Maps by Hal Jespersen

Touring the Battlefield   X

Seven Days' Battle   XIV

Battle of Beaver Dam Creek   26

Battle of Gaines's Mill, 2:30 p.m.   38

Battle of Gaines's Mill, 7 to 8:30 p.m.   52

Savage's Station   66

Seven Days's Battle   74

Frayser's Farm   92

Kemper's Attack   94

Attacks in the Center   96

The Final Attacks   98

Battle of Malvern Hill (First Phase)   106

Battle of Malvern Hill (Second Phase)   116

Battle of Malvern Hill (Third Phase)   118

On the morning of June 30, Theopholis Holmes placed his troops at New Market Heights, "A position of great natural strength." (dc)

Acknowledgments

I owe a debt of gratitude to several people who were of great help in writing this book.

Chris Mackowski provided encouragement and guidance to the project, which was greatly appreciated. Chris is a talented writer and editor, and I was grateful for his suggestions. I'm thankful, too, to publisher Theodore Savas at Savas Beatie, who made this book possible.

The talented Andy Welch took many of the images. Hal Jespersen, whose work has become widely appreciated, created the maps. Hal always does excellent work and is very professional and patient.

Robert E. L. Krick once again opened his amazing library to me. Bob is extremely generous with the resources at his disposal. Anyone doing serious research on the war in the Richmond area must visit Bob's library at the Richmond National Battlefield Park (RNBP) headquarters.

Mark Wilcox wrote the appendix on Stuart's Ride. Mark is a park ranger with the RNPB and also is a great friend and fellow battlefield explorer.

Lastly, Bert Dunkerly provided assistance in any way possible. Bert has been very supportive of all of my projects, offering advice, helping to lead tours, introducing me to other historians and recommending speaking opportunities.

PHOTO CREDITS:
Author's collection (ac/dc); Civil War Trails (cwt); Doug Crenshaw (dc); Library of Congress (loc); Ashley Luskey (al); Chris Mackowski (cm); Richmond National Battlefield Park (rnbp); Virginia Historical Society (vhs); Andrew Welch (aw); Kris White (kw); Wikipedia Commons (wc); Mark Wilcox (mw)

For the Emerging Civil War Series

Theodore P. Savas, *publisher*
Chris Mackowski, *series editor*
Kristopher D. White, *chief historian*
Sarah Keeney, *editorial consultant*

Maps by Hal Jespersen
Design and layout by H.R. Gordon
Publication supervision by Chris Mackowski

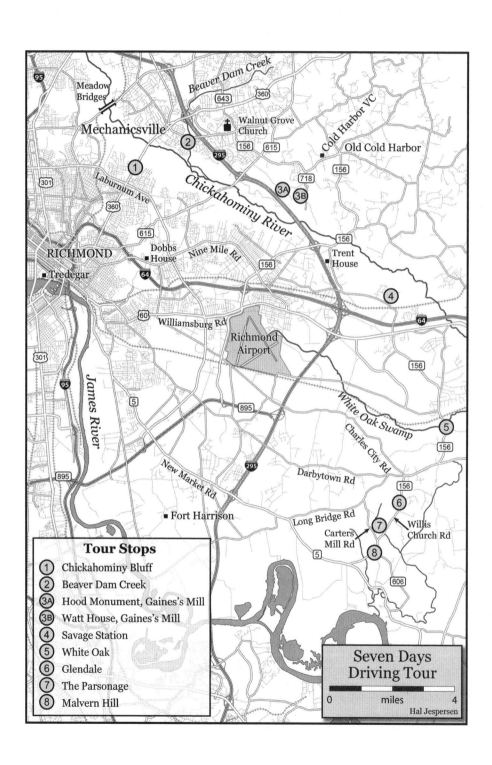

Meadow
Bridges

Mechanicsville

Walnut Grove
Church

Cold Harbor VC

Old Cold Harbor

Chickahominy River

Laburnum Ave

RICHMOND

Dobbs
House

Nine Mile Rd

Tredegar

Trent
House

James River

Williamsburg Rd

Richmond
Airport

White Oak Swamp

Charles City Rd

New Market Rd

Darbytown Rd

Fort Harrison

Long Bridge Rd

Willis
Church Rd

Carters
Mill Rd

Tour Stops

1. Chickahominy Bluff
2. Beaver Dam Creek
3A. Hood Monument, Gaines's Mill
3B. Watt House, Gaines's Mill
4. Savage Station
5. White Oak
6. Glendale
7. The Parsonage
8. Malvern Hill

Seven Days
Driving Tour

0   miles   4

Hal Jespersen

Touring the Battlefield

Because development has swelled outward from the city center, modern encroachment has swallowed many of the Seven Days' battlefields. Use extreme caution while following the tour. Roads along the first half of the tour, in particular, can be congested and busy; roads along the second half of the tour, while more rural, wind around several blind curves and hills.

The tour will follow the chronological order of the battle, and directions to each site will precede the discussion of each battle. The tour begins at Richmond National Battlefield Park's main visitor center, located at the site of the Tredegar Iron Works. From downtown, take Fifth Street until it stops at Tredegar Street, and turn right. The parking lot is on the right, just past the first building. Exhibits, films, and a helpful staff assist with orientation to the battlefields. Also on the site is the American Civil War Center, a private museum. A visit is recommended.

With the benefit of 20-20 hindsight, a National Park Service sign at Malvern Hill captures the feel of the Confederate assault there on July 1, 1862: "Madness." (cm)

Foreword

BY ROBERT M. DUNKERLY

One of the lesser-studied campaigns of the war, the Seven Days' Battles offers numerous insights for those interested in the progression of the war. The underlying theme, from any perspective, is a state of flux.

The summer campaign before Richmond occurred at a crucial time in the war, with political, economic, and social changes unfolding that would alter the character of the conflict and how it was waged. Perhaps the most important current was the rising tide of emancipation.

As Union troops entered the Peninsula counties and the environs of the capital city, they encountered large numbers of slaves who saw them as liberators. While the attitude of Union troops varied from zealously abolitionist to indifference to hostility, the contraband issue became one that military commanders in the field, and policy makers in Washington, had to address.

Although Antietam is usually associated with the Emancipation Proclamation, the groundswell leading to that event occurred in the spring and summer, in large part as the Army of the Potomac found itself entangled in this difficult and controversial issue.

The economies of both nations also geared up for a larger war effort. The Union government was wresting with how to manage uncooperative Southern civilians, guerillas, and a host of other administrative details that spring. The conciliatory

To call the Chickahominy a river is a bit of a misnomer. When the water is high, it more resembles fast-running floodwater; when it's low, it's a meandering morass. Either way, it poses significant challenges to an army that seeks to cross. (dc)

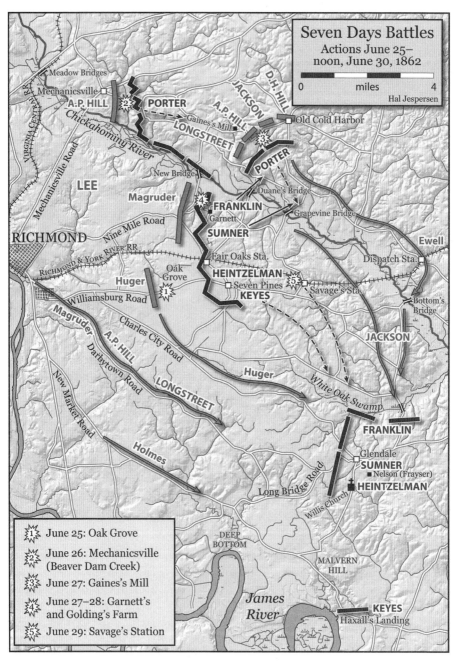

Seven Days Battles
Actions June 25–
noon, June 30, 1862

0   miles   4

Hal Jespersen

June 25: Oak Grove

June 26: Mechanicsville
(Beaver Dam Creek)

June 27: Gaines's Mill

June 27–28: Garnett's
and Golding's Farm

June 29: Savage's Station

SEVEN DAYS' BATTLE—The road system from Richmond radiated outward like the spokes of a wheel. As McClellan tried to shift his army from the Chickahominy to the James, Lee tried to send Confederate forces smashing into the flank of the Federal army as it intersected these roads. Time after time, Lee had difficulty getting his divisions into the right place at the right time for a decisive blow, although McClellan's harried columns found themselves fighting rearguard actions during their entire movement.

policy was clearly not working, and it gradually became clear that harsher measures were needed as Union armies operated in the South. The Confiscation Act, for example, is one clear sign that property, including slaves, could be forfeited by those who took up arms against the government. Popular opinion in the north was gradually moving towards accepting a tougher policy needed to wage the war.

Changes in policy were also happening in Jefferson Davis's administration. That spring, the Confederacy instituted a draft (the first in American history), enacted price controls, muffled the press, and took other steps into uncharted territory to manage its war effort.

The military actions in Hanover and Henrico Counties reveal that the armies were also in transition. General Robert E. Lee inherited an army with an awkward command structure. Stonewall Jackson's force, recently arrived from the Valley, had little time to properly integrate with the Army of Northern Virginia. Jackson's command, a wing, was not officially a corps, and would not be designated as such until after the campaign. Jackson acted largely independently, and Lee treated his command that way during the campaign.

General John B. Magruder's command, formerly the Army of the Peninsula, had recently been absorbed by the Army of Northern Virginia. Magruder commanded two divisions as well as his own division directly. It was an awkward, pseudo corps arrangement and likely to lead to command and control issues (which it did).

Lee himself was new to command on such a scale. In fact, only a handful of officers on either side had any experience coordinating the movements of large forces. For Lee, it was learning on the job, and there would be many bumps in the road.

Staff work was lacking, and communication was poor. The results created challenges in coordination throughout the campaign, hindering Lee's ability to achieve his objectives. While the Union army was driven away from Richmond, it was not destroyed, as Lee intended.

On the Union side, although the army's structure was better, there were many close calls and near disasters, largely due to the inattention of Gen. George B. McClellan to properly communicate with his corps commanders. Only good cooperation among his subordinates averted catastrophe. Nearly all of the Union commanders also ineffectively used their cavalry.

The logistical systems of both armies were learning rapidly, gearing up for what was quickly escalating into a conflict of scale and duration that neither anticipated (or were ready for). Supply, transport, engineering, medical, and other support services were tested—and for the most part performed well.

The battles themselves reveal learning at the company, regimental, and brigade level. Ineffective frontal assaults, lack of coordination, deficient scouting, and poor use of artillery and cavalry all defined many of the battles at the small-unit level. By the fall of 1862, they would all be professionals at skirmishing, scouting, maneuvering, fortifying, and assaulting. However, he armies fighting on the Peninsula were not the same armies that would fight at Antietam, Chancellorsville, or Gettysburg. Rather, those lessons were learned in the spring and summer along the swampy Chickahominy. These were armies learning as they went: they were in the process of becoming. Everything that the armies learned of fighting, marching, and maneuvering in the field, they learned, for the most part, in the Seven Days'.

Seven Pines was the largest battle in the eastern theater up to that time. Then Gaines's Mill was larger than that. Then came a dizzying pace of engagements, culminating with Malvern Hill, the only battle in which the majority of both armies were on the field.

We will see many junior officers who will rise to prominence and reach their full potential later (or displayed the attributes that likely *would* have flowered had not other events intervened). Meade, Hooker, Kearny, Reynolds, Custer, Birney, Couch, Hancock, Griffin, and Upton all showed promise for the Union. For the Confederates, Gordon, Hood, R. H. Anderson, Gregg, Hampton, Early, and Ewell would soon rise above their lower grades and commands.

The Seven Days' not only changed the character of the war—with the growing push for emancipation and new focus on a harsher policy towards Southern civilians—it extended the war. It could have resulted in a Union victory that summer with Richmond's fall. It demonstrated, brutally and clearly, that the war would be a long one. Although First Manassas is often seen the as the battle that broke the "quick war" and "one battle" mentality, soldiers' diaries are filled with expectations of one big battle at Richmond to determine the war. That persistent myth finally died a hard death in the swamps in the summer of 1862. Private John Faller of the 7th Pennsylvania Reserves wrote home, "If anyone tells you that the rebels will not fight, just tell them to come down to this neck of the country and try them on."

Lastly, each of the Seven Days' Battles presents a distinctive opportunity to study a specific engagement. Each had unique topography: open-field combat, woods and swamps, or hilly terrain. Road networks—points of access and egress— varied. While the Confederates were generally the aggressor, Union counterattacks played significant roles in each battle. The ebb and flow of combat created fluid situations in these engagements. Studied independently, they each offer insights for both historians and modern military commanders.

ROBERT M. DUNKERLY *is a historian, award-winning author, and speaker actively involved in historic preservation and research. Co-author of the ECWS book No Turning Back: A Guide to the 1864 Overland Campaign, Bert is a Park Ranger at Richmond National Battlefield Park.*

Norfolk had fallen and the *Virginia* had been scuttled. Federal gunboats were heading up the James River, with only the fortifications at Drewry's Bluff standing in their way. Joseph Johnston's army was retreating towards Richmond. President Jefferson Davis summoned his advisor Robert E. Lee to a cabinet meeting and asked where the Confederate army might make a stand if driven from Richmond. Lee, well known for his self-control, had tears in his eyes as he passionately replied, "Richmond must not be given up; it shall not be given up!"

W 7

FAIR OAKS STATION

This intersection of the Richmond and York River Railroad with the Nine Mile Road became one of Henrico County's best-known landmarks during the Civil War. Fair Oaks Station lay on the north side of the junction. As part of Gen. Joseph E. Johnston's Confederate attack at Seven Pines on 31 May 1862, his troops under Brig. Gen. Richard H. Anderson passed here as they assaulted the Union right. On 29 June 1862, an innovative Confederate artillery piece was pushed past the intersection by a locomotive and used during the Battle of Savage's Station. It consisted of a siege gun mounted on a flatcar behind a shield of rails. This was the first use of railroad artillery in warfare.

DEPARTMENT OF HISTORIC RESOURCES, 1994

W 10

SECOND DAY A SEVEN PINES

Prologue

It's a quiet little town now, Seven Pines, with its eastern edge touching the Richmond International Airport. A few scattered signs indicate that something important once happened here, although not many people notice as they go about their day. But it wasn't always such a calm, peaceful place.

On May 31, 1862, Gen. Joseph E. Johnston, commander of the Confederate forces defending Richmond, launched an attack against Maj. Gen. George B. McClellan's massive Army of the Potomac at Seven Pines, only a few miles outside of the Confederate capital. Johnston had hoped to unhinge McClellan's army before it could gather enough force to make its final assault on Richmond. But the battle did not go as planned. It was not well managed, staff work was poor, and troops were often in the wrong place at the wrong time. Thousands never got into the action at all.

That evening, Johnston rode down the Nine Mile Road toward the sound of the firing to get a better look at the situation. About 200 yards from the road's intersection with the York River Railroad, he stopped to talk to a member of his staff. Suddenly, a musket ball hit him in the shoulder, and then a fragment of an artillery shell struck him in the chest, knocking him from his horse. Subordinates had to carry him from the field. It seemed a repeat of the recent events

In one of the most significant turning points of the war, Joseph Johnston was wounded at Fair Oaks Station, leading to the ascension of Robert E. Lee to command of Confederate forces in the east. Lee would not only throw back Union forces but change the entire tempo of the war in Virginia. (cm)

LEFT: The one-time hero of Manassas, "Old Joe" Johnston saw his stock plummet in the spring of 1862 as he backpeddled his way up the James River Peninsula, away from an advancing Army of the Potomac. (loc)

RIGHT: As a commander of Confederate forces in Virginia, Gustavus Woodson Smith is like George Lazenby of the James Bond films—there for such an unextraordinary flash that people almost entirely forget him. (loc)

at Shiloh when Gen. Albert Sidney Johnston was killed. Now another leading Confederate commander was down.

President Jefferson Davis received word of General Johnston's wounding, and he rode to meet Gen. G. W. Smith, who now commanded the Confederate army around Richmond. Davis spent time discussing Smith's plans, then rode away with his military advisor, Robert Edward Lee. Not liking what he had heard from Smith, Davis made one of his most fateful decisions. He turned to Lee and said, "General Lee, I shall assign you command of this army. Make your preparations as soon as you reach your quarters. I shall send you the order when we get to Richmond."

After checking out the action by the railroad, Johnston turned back up the road and came to the Hitchcock house, seen here in a postwar photo, 200 yards away. There, he suffered two injuries: one from a stray piece of shrapnel and another from a bullet. (ac/dc)

Today, a former auto parts store sits on the site of Johnston's wounding. (dc)

One can only imagine Lee's thoughts as he continued riding. He had never commanded a large army in combat, and now the very existence of the Confederate capital, and the Confederacy itself, would depend on his actions.

The next day, June 1, Smith continued the battle to no avail. Around two o'clock in the afternoon Gen. Robert E. Lee rode up to Smith's headquarters and announced that he had been placed in command.

It was the dawn of the Army of Northern Virginia.

Prelude to the Seven Days

CHAPTER ONE

SPRING 1862

The spring of 1862 was a dark time for the Confederacy. Not yet a year past its victory at Bull Run, it had suffered a string of defeats that threatened to bring it to its knees. In the west, Island No. 10 had fallen along the Mississippi, and Forts Henry and Donelson had been lost in Tennessee. The strategic cities of Nashville and Corinth had fallen. At Shiloh, the Confederates suffered yet another defeat, and Gen. Albert Sidney Johnston, one of the South's most promising military leaders, had been killed. New Orleans, the Confederacy's largest city, had been captured. In the east, Fort Macon had been taken, and Union troops had landed on North Carolina's outer banks. In mid-March, a Federal army under Gen. George B. McClellan had landed on the tip of the Virginia Peninsula near Fort Monroe and had begun a slow, methodical march towards Richmond. In its wake, Confederates had abandoned their seaport and naval yard in Norfolk and had scuttled its famous ironclad, the *Virginia*. The survival of the Confederacy was very much in doubt.

During that same time, McClellan had taken the Union mob that had fled from the defeat in July 1861 at Manassas and crafted it into a massive, well-drilled, well-supplied modern army—to which he had added a large number of modern field artillery as well as many heavy siege

Site of the Confederacy's primary artillery foundry, the Tredegar Iron Works is now the home of the Richmond National Battlefield Park's main visitor center, as well as the American Civil War Museum. (dc)

Part of the Seven Pines Battlefield, Williamsburg Road in Sandston illustrates the lack of preservation efforts common during much of the twentieth century. (dc)

guns. The months passed. As President Abraham Lincoln, Secretary of War Edwin Stanton, and a significant number of legislators watched the army's progress, their frustration began to mount from what they saw as a resistance of McClellan to make use of the force he had built. A vote to censure the general narrowly failed to pass in the Senate. Constantly, exhortations encouraged McClellan to move. It was said, "The fire in the rear is a terrific one." Regardless, the general would move in his own time. Ever confident, he told a reporter from the *New York World*, "I believe we are on the eve of the success for which we have been so long preparing."

Then, instead of riding south from the Manassas area as everyone had expected, McClellan had moved his army to the Virginia peninsula, near Fort Monroe and Norfolk. McClellan then headed slowly up the peninsula toward Richmond. As McClellan advanced, Confederate commander Joe Johnston pulled back from his position at Manassas and shifted to the east of Richmond to face the Federals. McClellan expected to arrive outside of the Confederate capital with his 100,000-plus-man army and to be joined by a corps under Gen. Irvin McDowell, who would move south from the Fredericksburg area. McClellan would crush the Confederate defense by both this move and by using his heavy siege artillery.

The Federal commander established his supply base at White House on the Pamunkey River,

This national cemetery in Sandston was one of several created by the U.S. government in the Richmond area to deal with the Federal war dead. (dc)

This sign about the Seven Days' is located at the Sandston Library, within a few hundred feet of Casey's Redoubt from the battle. (dc)

planning to utilize the Richmond & York River Railroad to move supplies and heavy artillery forward. There seemed to be only one complication: his army was bisected by the Chickahominy River.

"Calling the Chickahominy a river is an insult to rivers!" one Richmond historian has said. At most times he is right. However, at any given time it can be a serious obstacle to an army in motion. In most places no more than 20 feet wide and a few feet deep, frequently, though, it breaks into other branches. It is a morass of soft ground, scrub vegetation, voracious insects, and snakes. On either side, long stretches of soft bottomland eventually rise into steep bluffs. Moving men across it would be a nasty business, and moving wagons and artillery would be impossible without bridges. When rains come and swell the river, bridges could be washed out, further complicating attempts to traverse it.

The Sandston Library sits on the location of McClellan's main line during the battle. (dc)

After pulling back from Seven Pines, McClellan gave Confederates desperately needed time to reorganize. After the wounded were gathered, Lee ordered a strengthening of the city's defenses while he formulated a new strategy. (loc)

Meticulous McClellan's strategy required that a substantial force be kept north of the river for a few reasons. First, he had to protect his base of supply at White House, as well as the York River Railroad. Additionally, he needed troops in the Mechanicsville area to reach out to McDowell's corps as it arrived from Fredericksburg. To deal with the risk created by the Chickahominy, he ordered engineers to build a series of bridges.

Having a force in Mechanicsville produced a further benefit: it gained control of the New Bridge, which had elevated runways that were not quickly washed out by the swelling of the river. The bridge would provide excellent access to the south side as McClellan's army advanced west on Nine Mile Road towards Richmond.

For the Confederate commander, McClellan's transitory troop dispositions appeared to offer a slim opportunity. The Federals were in the outskirts of Richmond, and Johnston realized that he could not hold off the Army of the Potomac indefinitely, particularly if it could get close enough to the city to pound it with siege artillery.

Abandoning Richmond could be fatal. Not only was the government housed there, but it

The Dabbs house is now a Henrico County museum. Located at 3812 Nine Mile Road, just off Interstate 64 (Nine Mile Road east), it has been modified over time and is larger than the historic building. It houses exhibits plus a research library. The museum is open Wednesday through Sunday from 9 a.m. to 5 p.m. Interestingly, its basement was modified into a Cold War bunker, but the basement is not open to the public at this time. The museum's phone number is (804) 652-3406. GPS: N 37 58.459, W 77 36.255 (dc)

was also the seat of major Confederate wartime industries, such as the Tredegar Iron Works and the Virginia Manufactory of Arms.

On May 27, Johnston received word that a Federal force had driven the Confederates from Hanover Court House in preparation for meeting up with McDowell. The Confederate commander had to do something to knock McClellan off balance and possibly drive him down the Peninsula. Time was of the essence.

Studying the terrain, Johnston realized how the Chickahominy could flood; if that happened, McClellan could experience great difficulty in moving his troops across it to meet an attack. Johnston planned to take advantage of this potential advantage and launch an assault.

At first, Johnston planned to attack the Federals at Mechanicsville in order to prevent them from linking up with McDowell, who was rumored to be moving south. General Johnston then received unexpected and welcome news: McDowell had reversed direction (his movement south had only been a diversion). Johnston decided to attack south of the river with two-thirds of his army. The night before the battle, he received a gift in the form of a storm that would swell the Chickahominy. Conditions appeared to be ideal for his offensive!

As is so often the case, appearances can be deceiving and plans can go awry. The attack was badly bungled, and the Federal troops held on. One of the bridges McClellan, the former civil engineer and railroad executive, had built allowed reinforcements to arrive from the north side at a critical moment. At the end of the first day of the battle of Seven Pines—or Fair Oaks, as it was also called—Johnston was wounded, the Confederate attack had failed, and McClellan was poised at the gates. It was one of the darkest hours of the Confederacy.

At The Tredgar Iron Works

The Richmond National Battlefield Park Visitor Center stands at the industrial heart of the Confederacy. While numerous other manufacturing facilities were located in Richmond, Tredegar was the South's principal iron foundry. Before the war, it produced rails and locomotives, spikes, horseshoes, and iron products of every description. It also made cannons for the United States government. During the war, Tredegar forged 1,099 artillery pieces—half of the total produced throughout the Confederacy.

Following the war, the foundry reopened and continued to operate until the 1950s. In addition to a wide array of other iron goods, it produced artillery shells for the United States and Great Britain during World Wars I and II.

The visitor center has a knowledgeable staff, many artifacts, movies on Tredegar and on the campaigns around Richmond, and a bookstore. A fully outfitted 12-pounder Napoleon gun stands on the second floor—feel free to ask for a demonstration on how it worked. You should definitely take the time to enjoy the site. Also,

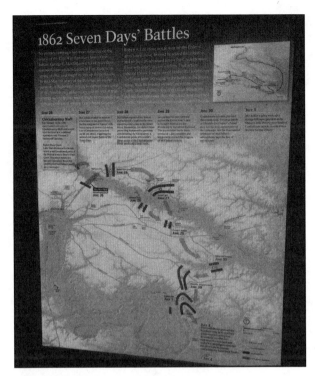

1862 Seven Days' Battles

The series of battles that Lee would initiate would drive the Federal army away from the gates of Richmond. The National Park Service installed a map of the Seven Days' at the first tour stop, Chickahominy Bluffs. (dc)

the American Civil War Center is next door, so be sure to check that out. Two museums in one stop—hard to beat!

➤ TO STOP 1: CHICKAHOMINY BLUFFS

To reach the first stop on the tour, take a left out of the Tredegar parking lot. Make your first left, and proceed up Fifth Street to the third traffic light, Cary Street. Turn right. Quickly get into the left lane and, in two blocks, turn left on Seventh Street. Stay on Seventh Street until you pass the Richmond Coliseum (on your left). Ahead you will see an array of highway signs. Choose 64 East. Once on 64 East, you will cross a bridge. The first pair of exits will be for 360. Take the East-Mechanicsville exit. You will now be on 360; follow for 1.9 miles. You will eventually cross Laburnum Avenue. When you pass the Hardees's restaurant (on your right), keep an eye out for the Chickahominy Bluffs tour spot on your right. It's easy to miss, so look carefully! This is your first stop.

The road past Chickahominy Bluff can be busy, so keep an eye out for the signs. (cm)

Lee Takes Command

CHAPTER TWO

JUNE 1, 1862

The Southern army that General Lee inherited on June 1 was not familiar to him. It was basically a young army, and its organization and leadership had not quite settled in. Lee did not know its commanders well: James Longstreet, Daniel Harvey Hill, Ambrose Powell Hill, John B. Magruder, Benjamin Huger, and James Ewell Brown "Jeb" Stuart. It would take a little time to determine their abilities, so for the time being, he would have to go with them.

Just below these commanders was a crop of men of unusual talent who would be heard from in the years ahead—men like John B. Hood, Richard Ewell, Jubal Early, and Richard Anderson. Others suggested potential, as well: Robert Rodes, Joseph Kershaw, Cadmus Wilcox, Maxcy Gregg, William Mahone, John B. Gordon, Lewis Armistead, E. Porter Alexander, Wade Hampton, Fitz Lee and more.

Also at Lee's disposal was one general he *was* fairly familiar with: Maj. Gen. Thomas "Stonewall" Jackson.

Jackson was a strange man. Eccentric by nature, he was also deeply Calvinistic. He was extremely secretive, and he often left his immediate subordinates in the dark concerning his plans. Prior to the war, he had taught at the Virginia Military Institute, although his methods were not particularly effective. Some of his students even called him "Tom Fool." But the man could fight.

Confederates created earthworks at Chickahominy Bluffs in 1862 and improved them as the war progressed. The works would continue around much of Richmond. (cm)

LEFT: James Longstreet would emerge from the Seven Days as one of Lee's most trusted commanders. Lee would eventually name him second-in-command of the Army of Northern Virginia. (loc)

RIGHT: After taking command of the army on June 1, Robert E. Lee earned the nickname "Granny Lee" from some of his soldiers because he concentrated on Richmond's defenses instead of assaulting the Army of the Potomac. Over time, however, he would become the Confederacy's most effective and beloved commander. (loc)

While President Davis's military advisor, Lee had studied the situation in Virginia carefully. As Johnston moved south to challenge McClellan, the remaining Confederate troops in Northern Virginia and the Shenandoah Valley were greatly outnumbered by the Union commands of Nathaniel Banks, James Shields, John Fremont, and Irvin McDowell. The two largest Confederate concentrations were the commands of Jackson and Maj. Gen. Richard S. Ewell. Others were sprinkled about, but at significant distances. Lee had to counter the serious Federal threat and reasoned that Jackson was his best bet to do it. He sent Ewell's small army to the Valley, giving Jackson a combined force of about 17,000 men. On paper, that was far from enough to do the job assigned to it.

At first, Lee intended to have Jackson keep the Federals in the Valley off balance and prevent them from seizing all of it. If they conquered the Valley, they could seriously disrupt the Confederate supply line. Should they join together under McDowell and come to Richmond, McClellan could potentially have 150,000 men just outside the Confederate capital. In a series of brilliant movements, Jackson proceeded to bewilder Fremont, Banks, and Shields in what became the legendary Valley Campaign.

Lee paid careful attention, and as May progressed, he became more and more convinced that Jackson's activities were also keeping McDowell from moving south. He was correct. In Washington,

Abraham Lincoln became alarmed at the potential threat Jackson presented to the Northern states and potentially to the capital, and kept McDowell's force at Fredericksburg, just in case he was needed to fend off a Confederate incursion.

To further feed Lincoln's fears, Lee sent the brigades of Brig. Gen. Alexander Lawton and Brig. Gen. William H. Chase Whiting, with a total of 8,000 men, to reinforce Jackson. It was done so that there was no secrecy, "[k]nowing the news would reach the enemy and induce the belief that Jackson was to be pushed north." Not only was Lincoln deceived, but it also convinced McClellan—who needed little persuasion—that he faced a massive Southern army near Richmond. How else could Lee possibly spare these troops when his capital was in imminent danger?

* * *

After taking command of the Confederate army around Richmond, several things became clear to Lee. As Johnston had before him, he realized he could not allow McClellan time to mass his numerically superior army at the capital's doorstep. Even more importantly, McClellan must be prevented from bringing up his massive heavy artillery, with which he could shell the city. But how could the Confederates prevent that?

Lee knew that, to be effective, the army needed discipline, and to fight, it needed better logistical support. He tackled both with great energy. He strove to better feed and supply the army, and in order to eliminate the favoritism created by elected commands, he began stocking it with men of ability and potential. He had a keen eye for a good soldier.

Lee also made what was considered, at the time, to be one of his most controversial decisions: he ordered his troops to construct a line of strong fortifications outside of the city. At first, soldiers and the press took to calling him the "King of Spades" and "Granny Lee." They thought that it was not dignified to hide behind a wall of dirt. Lee ignored his critics. The works would provide two critical benefits. First, of course, they would protect his army and make the greatest possible use of his numerically

"Stereo" images, such as this
view of the sleepy village of
Mechanicsville, were created
to provide a 3-D effect,
which at times can be quite
stunning. (loc)

"Stereo" images, such as this view of the sleepy village of Mechanicsville, were created to provide a 3-D effect, which at times can be quite stunning. (loc)

inferior force: fewer men could cover more ground when behind earthworks. This led to the second, and equally important benefit: by needing fewer men to protect his lines, Lee could take a large portion out to use as an attacking force. The Confederacy would soon see the wisdom of his actions.

Not everyone was underwhelmed by Lee's actions. Porter Alexander, who would rise to fame as an outstanding artillery officer, rode with a Joseph Ives, a member of President Davis's staff. Alexander worried that all of the time taken to build the fortifications was allowing McClellan the opportunity to gather his forces and prepare an attack. He asked his companion if Lee had the audacity to attack the numerically superior foe. To this Ives replied, "Alexander, if there is one man in either army, Confederate or Federal, head and shoulders above every other in *audacity*, it is Gen. Lee! His name might be Audacity. He will take more desperate chances and take them quicker than any other commander in this country, North or South; and you will live to see it, too."

Well aware that his opponent outnumbered him, the Confederate commander did everything possible to augment his force. Units were brought up from the south. Brigadier General Roswell S. Ripley's brigade arrived from South Carolina, and Brig. Gen. Robert Ransom, Jr., and Maj. Gen. Theophilus H. Holmes's units came from the Tar Heel state. Whiting and Lawton had been called up and sent to Jackson. If Lee included Jackson's force, Lee could have more than 90,000 men in Richmond. It would be the largest army he would ever field during the war.

Like Johnston, Lee reasoned that the best option would be to strike McClellan before McClellan's

This bridge over the Chickahominy was typical of several that spanned the river. (loc)

own preparations were complete. As he studied the best way to attack, he saw that the Federal left was solidly anchored by White Oak Swamp and the center was too strong. He then saw what he believed to be the Federal army's weakness: its supply line ran north of the Chickahominy to White House on the Pamunkey River. The railroad that the Federals required to bring up their heavy artillery also was on the northern side of the river. McClellan was totally dependent on this and, after Seven Pines, left one corps stationed north of the Chickahominy with about 30,000 men commanded by his most trusted subordinate, Fitz John Porter.

Lee wondered how far Porter's force extended to the Federal right. Was it properly secured? Could its flank be turned? To Lee, it made a tempting target, but he needed more information before he could formulate a plan. He needed answers, and he needed them now.

With an eye on discovering McClellan's weaknesses, Lee ordered Brig. Gen. Jeb Stuart, cavalry commander, to "Make a secret movement to the rear of the enemy now posted on the Chickahominy, with a view of gaining intelligence of his operations, communications, & c." The young Stuart took 1,200 of his troopers, including Col. Fitzhugh Lee and 1st Lt. John Singleton Mosby, and began heading around Porter's right. He discovered that Porter's flank was anchored on Beaver Dam

A National Park Service wayside at Chickahominy Bluffs shows Lee, Longstreet, and D. H. Hill observing the action on June 26. Lee actually posted himself across the street from where this sign is located. (dc)

Creek, but it was essentially "in the air," meaning that it was open to attack from its right flank. Stuart had found the opening Lee was looking for. (For a more complete treatment of Stuart's ride, see Appendix 1, "Eyes on the Peninsula: Stuart's Ride Around McClellan," by Mark Wilcox.)

The Confederate commander would take advantage of the Federal fears and dispositions. He felt confident that Jackson's Valley exploits had locked McDowell in at Fredericksburg. With Porter's right at risk, Lee would strike there. Taking benefit of the fortifications he had built, he would pull out the divisions of Maj. Gen. A. P. Hill, Maj. Gen. D. H. Hill, and Maj. Gen. James Longstreet. They would cross the Chickahominy and move against Porter's flank at Mechanicsville. Jackson would come down from the Valley and move behind Porter. Hopefully the Confederates would not only destroy Porter, but also be able to cut the Federal supply lines, forcing McClellan to abandon his position with few Confederate losses. It was a bold and audacious plan—one on which the Confederates staked everything.

From his headquarters at the Dabbs House, Lee sent word to Jackson, Longstreet, and the two Hills to come meet with him. Around three in the afternoon of June 23, D. H. Hill saw a tired, dusty soldier ride up, dismount, and walk into the house. It was Jackson. The previous night, the Valley commander had travelled 52 miles in the span of 14 hours—and that would prove to be only the beginning of his exhausting adventure.

The conference at the Dabbs House was the first meeting of the key men who would lead the army. All were graduates of West Point, all trained and experienced soldiers. While D. H. Hill would only be with Lee for a short time, Jackson would remain until his death at Chancellorsville nearly a year later. A. P. Hill would rise to corps command and fight on until he was killed outside of Petersburg in 1865. Longstreet became Lee's most trusted subordinate and would be with him at Appomattox.

Lee unveiled his plan. Realizing that they could not remain on the defensive and allow McClellan to retain the initiative, he said that they must attack—but how? Sharing the information Stuart had gathered, Lee proposed that they assault Porter's V Corps north of the river. Doing so would threaten or destroy McClellan's line of supply, force him out of his position, and either push him back down the Chickahominy or towards the James River. Lee outlined his bold plan to accomplish this result. The two Hills and Longstreet would take two-thirds of the army north of the river, leaving only Huger and Magruder to defend Richmond against the bulk of the Federal army.

Lee stood at this location, which is now private property, as he inspected the situation on June 26. The house sits along Rt. 360. (cm)

It was a risky move. Lee was betting the house that the lack of activity McClellan had demonstrated over the previous month would continue. If the Federals were to advance toward Richmond, Lee's offensive, and indeed the defense of the capital, would be in jeopardy. Would McClellan cooperate? It was a gamble Lee had to take. He did not have a lot of other choices.

The key to Lee's strategy was Jackson, who would bring his army from the Valley to Ashland, a sleepy town a few miles north of Richmond. From there, Jackson would sweep down behind Porter, threatening his rear and lines of communication and support. Brigadier General Lawrence O'Bryan (L. O. B.) Branch of A. P Hill's division, would be moved north of the city to a place called Half-Sink and make a connection with Jackson. Once Branch detected Jackson's approach, Hill

Alfred Waud identified this sketch as the bridge at Mechanicsville, but subsequent research has cast the identity of the image into doubt. (loc)

could cross at the Meadow Bridges and then turn towards Mechanicsville. By driving the Federals from that area, the bridge that traversed the Chickahominy would be uncovered, and D. H. Hill and Longstreet would be able to cross. With Jackson coming down in Porter's rear, the other three divisions would be able to sweep the Federals and drive them back. Once they passed the road leading to New Bridge, the danger to the army south of the river would be removed.

It was a daring plan that seemed to promise great results at a minimum cost. It would rely on clear understanding and execution. Lee then asked when Jackson might arrive so that they could begin the attack. The hero of the Valley replied that his army would be in position by June 25, but after receiving advice to give his men adequate time, he revised the date to June 26.

Lee left his field commanders to talk among themselves. Two days later he drafted General Order No. 75, detailing the plan. The die was cast.

At Chickahominy Bluffs

There is not a great deal to see here other than some preserved earthworks from the Confederate defensive line. As you approach the works, woods to your front block the view. In 1862, the ground would have been open, allowing a view of the action in the distance. Visitors used to be able to stand on an elevated viewing platform that looked out over the outermost works and down over the broad Chickahominy bottomlands, but with the tree-obstructed view, the Park Service removed the platform.

Lee actually watched the battle at Beaver Dam Creek (Mechanicsville) develop from across Route 360, which is now private property.

The Park Service has two particularly useful wayside exhibits here for orientation purposes. The first shows a map of the various battles that string together to make up the Seven Days'. The second shows the Richmond defenses, of which those atop the Chickohominy Bluffs are but a small part of.

When you continue on with the tour, the road will take you across the Chickahominy valley. When the water is low, the river runs maze-like across the marshy bottomlands; when it's high, the river flows in a single, strong stream. The area floods easily. Both armies knew the river made a formidable and unpredictable obstacle.

The Oak Grove site, mentioned in the next chapter, is no longer accessible. What once was the location of Oak Grove, French's Farm, and King's Schoolhouse is now the Richmond International Airport. The only evidence of the struggle that occurred there is an artillery position with a single cannon in it, as well as a few markers strewn about.

A National Park Service sign at Chickahominy Bluff maps out the Confederate defenses around Richmond. Lee earned the nicknames "Granny Lee" and "The King of Spades" for ordering the construction of the fortifications, but as a former engineer, he knew how invaluable the works would be. (cm)

McClellan Stirs

CHAPTER THREE

JUNE 23, 1862

Seven Pines presented George McClellan with a golden opportunity. The Confederate army was already disorganized after its failure at that battle. Added to that was the change in its leadership, and the insipient Army of Northern Virginia would not be in fighting shape for some time.

McClellan, however, was a cautious engineer. He had witnessed the bloody fighting in the Crimean War, and to his credit, he did not want to squander the lives of his men. On June 23, he wrote to his wife, "Every poor fellow that is killed or wounded almost haunts me!" Instead, he would do his best to win a battle of positions. He prepared to move forward slowly, readying the way to get his heavy artillery in place to shell the Confederate defenses and Richmond itself.

Additionally, a combination of the reports of the Pinkerton Agency, which headed his intelligence network, and his own paranoia, convinced General McClellan that the Southern army greatly outnumbered his own. Estimates of its strength ran from 150,000 to 200,000. That Lee had been able to send reinforcements to the Shenandoah Valley confirmed his fears. While not particularly concerned about Robert E. Lee's abilities, McClellan was very wary of the vast army he believed was facing him.

However, McClellan made perhaps his most fatal mistake in his estimate of Lee. On April 20, when Lee was President Davis's advisor, McClellan wrote to Lincoln: "Genl Robt Lee is in command in our front—Johnston is *under him!* I learn that there has been quite a struggle on the subject between

From Mechanicsville, McClellan sent his army away from the York River and toward the James following several routes, including the Old Cold Harbor Road, which led across Beaver Dam Creek. Today, a National Park Service footbridge spans the creek. (dc)

Known as "The Young Napoleon," George B. McClellan cultivated the comparison by posing with his hand in his jacket, similar to a pose the French general once made popular. (loc)

Davis & his Congress, Davis insisting upon Johnston. I prefer Lee to Johnston—the former is *too* cautious & weak under grave responsibility—personally brave & energetic to a fault, he yet is wanting in moral firmness when pressed by heavy responsibility & is likely to be timid & resolute in action."

During the first part of June, the weather did not favor Federal offensive movements. Rains had turned the roads to muddy quagmires, and moving heavy equipment was very difficult, if not impossible. McClellan had his engineers concentrate on building bridges, approaches, and roads.

By the middle of the month, the rains had passed and the roads were drying. In the meantime, however, the Army of the Potomac was melting from the heat and the diseases prevalent in the swampy area. Every day McClellan waited, his army grew weaker. Furthermore, as the month wore on, it became more and more apparent that McDowell's force was not coming down from Fredericksburg, no matter how much McClellan petitioned for it. Confederate deserters, escaped slaves, and spies began to indicate that Jackson was leaving the Valley and would be heading for Brig. Gen. John Fitz Porter's flank. Time was running out; McClellan would have to move.

Ironically, the timing of McClellan's attack coincided nearly perfectly with Lee's planned move, unbeknownst to either. McClellan's focus centered on getting his heavy artillery in position up the Nine Mile Road, near a place called Old Tavern (present day Highland Springs). On June 15, he wrote to his wife, "If we gain that the game is up for Secesh." From this point, he could "shell the city & carry it by assault." He would make it "mainly an artillery contest—I think I can bring some 200 guns to bear & sweep everything before us."

While the Union general told his wife he expected to move by June 17 or 18, he continued to procrastinate, making sure everything was prepared down to the smallest detail. It would be June 25 before he was ready.

McClellan planned to seize the ground to the south of Old Tavern first, with units from Brig. Gen. Samuel P. Heintzelman's III Corps making the assault from the left. Brigadier General Edwin V. Sumner's II Corps would then approach the

tavern from the center, while Brig. Gen. William B. Franklin's VI Corps would strike on Sumner's right.

Heintzelman sent forward units from Joseph Hooker's and Phil Kearny's divisions. These were two of the army's hardest fighters and most confident brigadier generals. Their immediate objective would be a small area south of the Williamsburg Road known as Oak Grove (the future site of the Richmond International Airport). The fight was not a significant affair—unless you were involved in it—and Federals gained little. Total casualties for both sides were roughly 1,000 men, and for that, Federals gained only a few hundred yards. Old Tavern would not be theirs this day.

McClellan was receiving messages that seemed to confirm the approach of Jackson. In his official report, he stated that on the 24th, he received word that Jackson's entire army was at Fredericks Hall and "that his intention was to attack our right flank and rear, in order to cut off our communications the White House and throw the right wing of our army into the Chickahominy." The next day, while the fighting raged at Oak Grove, McClellan received further confirmation of Jackson's advance. He immediately set out for Porter's headquarters and

Sketched just before the Seven Days', McClellan views the horizon towards the hamlet of Mechanicsville. (loc)

White House Landing served as McClellan's massive supply base on the Pamunkey River. The location of this base, once thought ideal, would create a major problem for McClellan in late June. (loc)

made preparations for defense. Rumors swirled that Pierre Gustave Toutant Beauregard, the renowned brigadier general, had come east and joined his army with Lee's. Convinced that he was facing at least "double my numbers," and confident of his officers and men, McClellan decided to "await the bursting of the coming storm."

He would not have long to wait.

Lee's note to Jefferson Davis the next day highlighted his unease about the affair at Oak Grove. "I fear from the operations of the enemy yesterday that our plan of operations has been discovered to them," he wrote. He believed the purpose of the Federal advance was to "discover whether our force on that front had been diminished."

What would Lee do? Most of his army was set to cross the Chickahominy, ready to strike Porter's right. Should he pull them back? If he didn't, could Major General Magruder and Major General Huger hold? With so much at stake, the answer seemed clear: the only chance he had to push back the Union force was to attack.

Lee would send roughly 55,000 men across the river, leaving about 29,000 to protect Richmond. Meanwhile, McClellan had 76,000 men south of the Chickahominy, poised six miles from the capital. Lee ordered the major generals to hold their positions "at the point of the bayonet if necessary."

Confederate troops retreated from Mechanicsville at the approach of Federal troops. On June 26, Confederates would return. (loc)

→ TO STOP 2: BEAVER DAM CREEK

Your next stop will be at Beaver Dam Creek. Turn right out of the parking lot at Chickahominy Bluffs. Stay in your right lane for 1.5 miles. You will cross a bridge over the Chickahominy River. After you cross, you will come to a traffic light. Proceed through it, and soon on your right, you will see a ramp with a sign for Rt. 156. Take this ramp. When you come to the stop sign, turn right. You will now be following the footsteps of some of A. P. Hill's men as they moved through Mechanicsville toward the Union lines at Beaver Dam Creek. At the time of the battle, this was open land populated by a few farms.

Richmond is surrounded by a web of waterways, like the Chickahominy River, which created logistical problems and defensive opportunities for both armies. (dc)

Proceed 0.7 miles through one traffic light. When safe and legal, drive straight through it. Soon, you will approach the bottom of a small hill, and on your right, you will see a sign for the Beaver Dam Creek battlefield. Turn in and drive to the parking lot.

GPS: N 37 59.567, W 77 35.379

BEAVER DAM CREEK

Confederate Troops, Pursuing Federals
Retreating eastward from Mechanicsville,
here came under Heavy Fire from across
Beaver Dam Creek and were Halted with
loss in the late Afternoon of June 20
1862.

8

A Creek in Mechanicsville

CHAPTER FOUR

JUNE 26, 1862

That night, the troops of Longstreet's and D. H. Hill's divisions headed for the bridge on the Mechanicsville Turnpike, preparing to cross as soon as A. P. Hill's men cleared the Federals out of Mechanicsville. A. P. Hill's division moved into position near the Meadow Bridges. Everything awaited the Valley army's arrival from Ashland.

Jackson's cavalry was running late, however. His command had not moved towards Richmond at the pace he had expected when he had promised to make the attack on June 26th.

Jackson always attempted to observe the Sabbath, and on the 22nd, he had called a halt. Around 1 a.m. on Monday, he mounted his horse and headed for the council with Lee at the Dabbs House. During his absence, his secretive nature worked against him. Leaving no one in charge who knew the destination of the planned movement, the army basically stagnated for another day. It moved at irregular paces, stretched out over 20 miles. On the 24th, it made good progress, but the rear of the army was still many miles behind. By nightfall most, but not all, of his army was near Ashland. However, it was supposed to be at Slash Church, several miles closer to Mechanicsville. The 25th was spent in pulling all of the army together, but it was still five miles short of Slash Church, leaving a greater distance to cover on the morrow than planned.

Fifty-nine markers dot the battlefields in Chesterfield, Henrico, and Hanover counties. The "Freeman monuments," written by noted Southern historian Douglas Southall Freeman, were installed in the 1920s after an ambitious fund-raising campaign by local battlefield boosters interested in promoting local tourism. (cm)

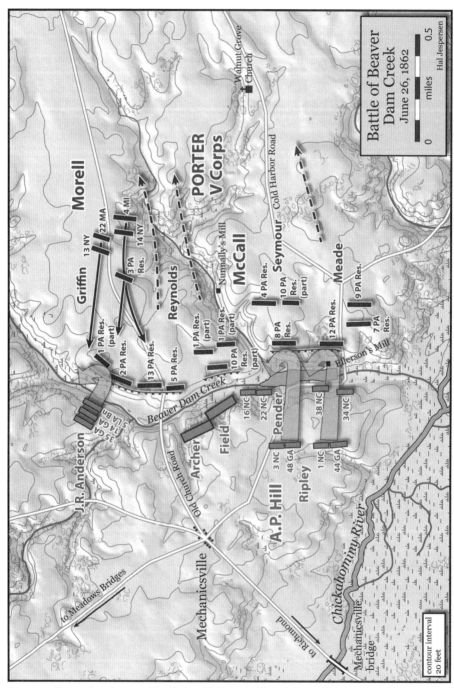

BATTLE OF BEAVER DAM CREEK—The Federal V Corps held high ground on the east side of Beaver Dam Creek, allowing it to fend off A. P. Hill, who attacked without expected support.

Around 3 a.m. on the 26th, Jackson's men started toward Porter's flank. Because he had not been in position at Slash Church, his attack would be several hours late.

As the sun rose that day, all seemed quiet to the Federals—yet on the western horizon, they began to see "vast clouds of dust" as Jackson's men advanced. Porter was not overly concerned about a direct attack by Lee from the direction of Mechanicsville, but "we did fear his attack, combined with one by Jackson on our flank." In preparation, Porter sent out detachments to create obstacles to Jackson's advance.

A solid division commander, Ambrose Powell Hill could at times be a bit too impetuous. He would rise to corps command after the death of Stonewall Jackson in 1863, but his aggressiveness as a division commander would translate poorly to the corps level. (loc)

The Pennsylvania Reserves division of Brig. Gen. George A. McCall laid in wait at a powerful natural position: behind the ridge of Beaver Dam Creek. The timber and thick brush on the Federal side of the bank concealed rifle pits and ample artillery. The ground around the small stream was marshy, and along the road from Mechanicsville ran a millrace, in some places waist deep. Cannons could dominate an attempt to cross the creek, making it an ideal defensive position. The banks were steep, with only two road crossing points: the bridge at Ellerson's Mill and the road to Old Church. Other units were stationed in Mechanicsville. At the Meadow Bridges, the divisions of brigadier generals George W. Morell and George Sykes, held in reserve.

Around 5 p.m., Stonewall Jackson reached Hundley's Corner, a few miles from John Fitz Porter's flank. Rather than continue to move behind Porter, Jackson had his men set up bivouac. The success of Lee's plan hinged on Jackson's movements, but he did not keep going. It was the beginning of a week of behavior that ran counter to the legend Jackson had created (and would continue to create in later actions).

In his report to Lee written the following February, Jackson did not indicate that he had done anything other than what was expected of him. Notoriously strict about following orders, it would seem that Jackson was not clear that he was to continue on that day. In his own report, Lee only mentioned that the attack was late due to the length of Jackson's march and the obstacles Jackson had encountered.

Ellerson's Mill sat along
Beaver Dam Creek. Behind it,
Federal troops would wait for
the Confederate attack. (loc)

In defense of Jackson, Lee's General Order No. 75, which outlined his plan for the attack, stated that Jackson was to advance on the road to Pole Green Church. Major General D. H. Hill was to cross the river and move to support Jackson. All four of the attacking divisions were to keep in communication with each other, moving in echelon and sweeping Porter. However, Jackson did not see D. H. Hill. Perhaps he was waiting for Hill before attacking, but we will likely never know. Added to this was the problem of poor maps of the area, a difficulty that would plague the Confederates for the remainder of the campaign.

Major General A. P. Hill, meanwhile, waited for any sign of Jackson, and as the afternoon wore on, Hill feared he was running out of time. Rather than compromise Lee's entire plan, Hill decided to take matters into his own hands. He ordered his light division to cross the Meadow Bridges and drive the Federals out of the small village of Mechanicsville. Jackson had to be close, Hill surmised; when Jackson arrived, he could join in the attack as planned.

As Hill's men approached the crossroads hamlet, the Union troops followed their instructions and retreated behind Beaver Dam Creek, joining the rest of McCall's

Today, the remains of the Ellerson's Mill foundation look like mounds of earth off in the forest. (cm)

division. Generals John Reynolds and Truman Seymour were instructed to place their brigades in the front line, with George Meade behind them.

Watching from across the Chickahominy, Lee saw A. P. Hill's advance and ordered D. H. Hill and then Longstreet to cross the river. He had little choice. His divisions were in position, and there was a danger that McClellan might strike for Richmond if the Confederates did not assault Porter *right then*. Where was Jackson?

A. P. Hill's Confederates drove through Mechanicsville and charged down the creek bank with a "shriek and yell," running out into the open. Their assault stretched from the right of today's

The Federals had one other advantage at Beaver Dam Creek, but it went unused: Thaddeus Lowe had an observation balloon available. It did not go up, though, so Federals had no aerial reconnaissance to warn of a pending attack. (loc)

battlefield park to the left across Cold Harbor Road and Old Church Road (now Route 360). McCall's Pennsylvanians were under cover and were ready for them.

On the far left, across Old Church Road, was Brig. Gen. Joseph Reid Anderson's brigade. The owner of the Tredegar Iron Works, the general had been trained at West Point and had offered his services as a Confederate field commander. Across the swamp from Anderson were the 2nd Pennsylvanian Reserves, with the 1st Reserves coming up in support. To Anderson's right, across the road, the brigades of generals James J. Archer and Charles W. Field advanced. As they descended a ridge, they saw the men of McCall's division. The Pennsylvanians had cut down trees to create clear fields of fire for their artillery. Not only would the Confederates attack in the open, they had to cross a swamp and, in one area, a millpond, while the Federals steadily fired upon the butternut soldiers from behind protective works. It was a strong position, one that the Confederates would not likely carry with Hill's division alone.

As they advanced, the Rebel attackers "gave a yell such as so many demons could make," but they were soon within range of rifle fire and canister. A particularly nasty weapon, canister was a can filled with small balls. The can would disintegrate when the gun was fired, violently spraying the balls out like a huge shotgun. The resulting carnage was terrible.

Holes would be blasted in lines and scores of men would be killed or mutilated with each blast. "We opened our terribly destructive fire upon them," a Federal artillerist said.

As the Confederates assaulted across Beaver Dam Creek, the topography presented challenges. (mbp)

The Confederate wounded screamed in agony. When the Southern soldiers got closer, the Union defenders loaded double charges, and even triples. Surviving that was not the end of the danger, though: men not hit with canister fire were slaughtered by the Pennsylvanians' rifles. It was a hopeless task.

As the Federal line extended near the swamp, the land began to level out by the bridge at Ellerson's Mill. There, A. P. Hill saw a chance of turning the enemy's left flank, and he ordered Dorsey Pender to strike. Cold Harbor Road made a sharp right turn and then a left, crossing by the mill. Pender's men advanced across the field and down the ridge toward the swamp—and then were greeted by a murderous crossfire.

A. P. Hill clearly required support, but what the army really needed was the turning movement by Jackson—yet the hero of the Valley campaign was nowhere in sight. The only troops immediately available were those of Brig. Gen. Roswell S. Ripley, who were in the advance of D. H. Hill's division, just then beginning to arrive. Ripley's men were ordered into the fray in an attempt to turn the Federal flank, but to no avail. Rather than attempt turning the flank, they advanced directly towards the millpond. "[M]y heart beat quick and my lips became dry, my legs felt weak and a prayer rose to my lips," one Southerner said. Such was the terror of facing the enemy's artillery and rifle fire.

Of the Confederate attackers, a Federal officer would write that their bodies lay "as thick as flies in a bowl of sugar." Confederate E. Porter Alexander summed it up glumly: "A more hopeless charge was never entered upon." One of Ripley's regiments, the 44th Georgia, lost 335 out of the 514 men who entered the battle.

Tactically, Lee's assault gained nothing. Only five brigades had been involved, with 11,000 men. The Federals, in a strong defensive position, outnumbered them with 14,000. A. P. Hill lost some 1,400 in the attack, while McCall suffered but 360

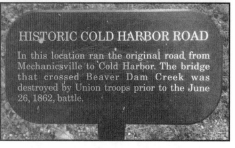

Signs mark the path of Cold Harbor Road at the time of the battle. (cm)

casualties. D. H. Hill would later lament, "We were lavish of blood in those days, and it was thought to be a great thing to charge a battery of artillery or an earth-work lined with infantry."

The Confederates benefitted little from their severe casualties. Without Jackson attacking Fitz Porter's right flank or rear, the Federal position was just too strong. Porter had not been trapped. Lee's first battle was a severe disappointment, and his army south of the river would be in peril if McClellan moved against it. It would be an anxious night.

Jackson, meanwhile, was only three miles away. It will remain a mystery why he did not send out scouts to find the positions of the other Confederates. Similarly, why did not Lee or Branch send horsemen out to find Jackson's cavalry? Its advance behind Porter would have been disastrous to the Federals, but for whatever reason, Stonewall Jackson did not join the fight.

Lee's plan was a bold, but complex one, and perhaps his army had not yet been ready for it. However, as flawed the Confederate move turned out to be, it would prove to be of significant strategic importance.

At Beaver Dam Creek (Mechanicsville)

At the end of the parking lot, a sign shows the perspective of a sketch of the Confederate assault.
(cm)

The condition of this battlefield has changed greatly since 1862. The area has been developed, and a modern highway, Route 295, cuts through it. Most of Beaver Dam Creek has become overgrown. As a result, Beaver Dam Creek Park is in somewhat poor condition owing to the effects caused by construction of the highway that runs through it. The Park Service property sits on the right end of the Confederate attack. The swamp in front of you is the field of battle.

As you face the swamp, turn around: the Confederates were coming from behind you. They stormed down into the bottomlands, across the creek, and assaulted the Federal position on the hill opposite. The scene was depicted in the woodcut used as the cover for this book. A Park Service wayside sign sits at roughly the location where the artist sketched the scene. In the subsequent 150 years, the course of the stream has meandered.

Note that the Confederate attack stretched to your left across Cold Harbor Road and beyond, across Route 360 (called "Old Church Road" at the time). The battle also traversed present day

A present-day view of the creek shows the remains of the millpond. (dc)

Route 295. The rear of the nearby shopping center and the Walmart were extensions of the Federal defensive positions.

Note that the wartime Cold Harbor Road followed the tour route. It made a right turn just as you did, and it crossed the swamp where the Park footbridge stands today. On the far side of the bridge, a small wayside sign points out the location of Ellerson's Mill. Only the foundation remains today, which can be hard to see when the foliage is in season.

Despite the terror and carnage of the day, there was one amusing story. Confederate President Jefferson Davis would display a penchant for

The Federal right flank is now a shopping center, and an interstate highway bisects the battlefield. (aw)

appearing on the Seven Days' battlefields to observe and even, at times, give orders. At Mechanicsville, Lee noticed Davis and some others on the field. Normally very cordial with the president, General Lee said sharply, "Who is this army of people and what are they doing here?"

Davis replied, "It is not my army, Gen.," to which Lee said, "It is certainly not *my* army, Mr. President, and this is no place for it!"

Understanding Lee's point, Davis then said, "Well, General, if I withdraw perhaps they will follow." He and his entourage rode off—but only until they were out of Lee's sight.

➤ TO STOP 3A: GAINES'S MILL

At the Walnut Grove intersection, seen here today, Jackson arrived from the left and turned left at the intersection. A. P. Hill turned right, heading down Cold Harbor Road. (aw)

As you leave Beaver Dam Creek, turn right, then proceed for 1.7 miles to a stoplight. Continue straight through the intersection. Notice the shopping center to your left that was part of the Federal position during the battle. On your right, you will see a sign that references Porter's withdrawal.

You will soon pass several white church buildings on your left. The farthest to the left is the historic Walnut Grove Church, where Lee, Jackson, and A. P. Hill met on the morning of June 27. Stop to read the signs, then continue to the stoplight and turn right.

This stoplight is an important reference point. Here, Jackson came from the left, turned and took the road straight ahead. A. P. Hill turned right, as you will do. This was his route to Gaines's Mill.

After you turn, travel for 2.8 miles. You will come to another stoplight—continue straight. You will soon head down a ravine. The ridge in front is where Lee expected Porter to make a stand. On the left is the site of Dr. Gaines's mill building, which no longer stands.

You will come to a sharp curve in the road. Do not take the curve, but instead drive straight. Soon you will see a monument to the 11th Mississippi on your left. Just past the monument, look to your right to see a dirt road with a single house on it. Go down this road a few hundred yards past the house. Park at the small turnaround at the end of the road. This is the site of the memorial to the Texas Brigade.

As you follow the driving tour, the site of Gaines's Mill sits to the left at the bottom of a dip in the road. The site is marked by a Virginia State Historical Commission sign and a Freeman marker. A small pullover allows motorists to stop at the site, but do so only when coming from the opposite direction and only with extreme caution because of the curve's poor sight lines. (cm)

Gaines's Mill: The First Phase

CHAPTER FIVE

JUNE 26-27, 1862

Late on June 26, General McClellan sent word to Washington of the army's "victory today . . . against great odds. . . . I almost begin to think we are invincible."

Inwardly, though, his thoughts were quite different. Although McCall's division had turned back the Confederate attack, McClellan decided that he must abandon his strategy. Rumors were flying concerning Stonewall Jackson's impending approach on the Union right flank, threatening the Federal supply line. As midnight passed, McClellan rode back to his headquarters at the Trent house, where he considered the situation. He quickly gave up any thoughts of laying siege to the Confederate capital and instead determined that he would move his base from the Pamunkey to the James, where it would be under the safety of the Federal gunboats.

In order to accomplish this, he would need time. McClellan ordered Porter to keep his V Corps north of the river for one more day but to pull back to a more defensible position, one where he could protect the bridges across the river and where Jackson could not turn his flank. To emphasize what he saw as a desperate situation, the Union commander cautioned his brigadier general: "You must hold your own until dark."

Porter received McClellan's orders around 2 a.m. on the 27th and immediately began pulling his

Longstreet led his troops down this road towards Gaines's Mill. It is a little-known dirt path today. (dc)

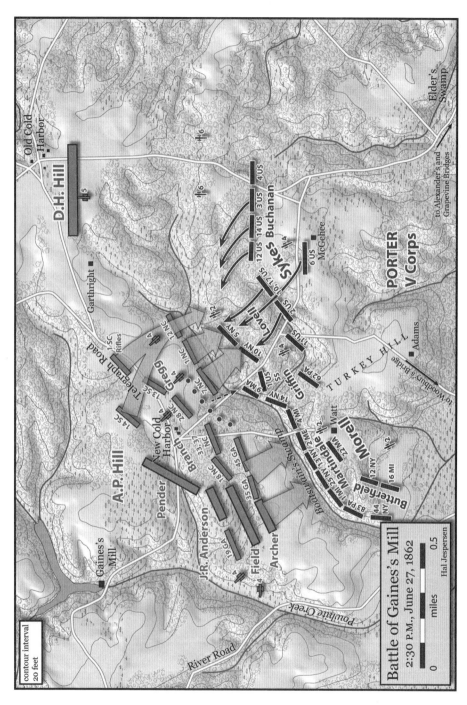

BATTLE OF GAINES'S MILL—Initial Confederate assaults swept up against a Federal defense three lines deep, posted atop a ridge that overlooks Boatswain's Creek. On the Federal right, George Skye's division moved in to bolster a shaky flank, allowing the V Corps to hold firm.

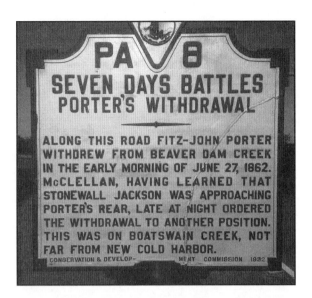

force back. He set up a preliminary defense along a steep ridge that ran near the home of Dr. William Gaines and extended past his mill.

Lee anticipated this, and he drew up a plan. With the divisions of A. P. Hill and Longstreet attacking directly towards Porter's assumed position, Jackson and D. H. Hill would move around Porter's right flank, farther east toward Old Cold Harbor. As Porter was forced to retreat because of the weight of the Confederate attack to his front, he would be driven into Jackson's waiting guns posted behind him. The road to the Federal supply base would be open. Porter's corps might even be destroyed.

Longstreet's and A. P. Hill's men approached the Federals by separate, parallel roads, and in so doing, uncovered the way to New Bridge, easing any fears Lee had for his force south of the river. He could now readily shuttle troops across to meet any threat.

But because his advance against Porter's front met scant resistance, Lee was puzzled. Where were the Federals? Why would they abandon this position so easily?

Porter had chosen a stronger location than his Gaines's Mill position. About a mile east, he stationed his army along a ridge behind a soggy, wooded area known as "Boatswain's swamp." It was a solid position, sitting on a high ridge behind the watercourse. With his left anchored on the farm

Fitz John Porter directed two defensive stands during the Seven Days', at Gaines's Mill and Malvern Hill. A steady commander, he was one of McClellan's favorites, but his career with the Army of the Potomac would be short-lived. (loc)

One of a couple state historical markers dedicated to Gaines's Mill, this sign stands near Walnut Grove Church. (dc)

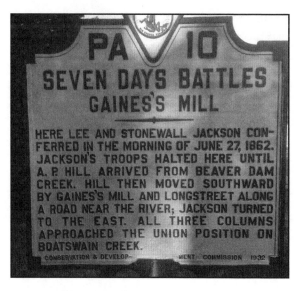

of Sarah Watt, Porter's line extended for nearly two miles to his right, across the Adams farm to a point hear Old Cold Harbor.

On Porter's left was Brig. Gen. George W. Morell's division, with Daniel Butterfield's, John Martindale's, and Charles Griffin's brigades, left to right. McCall was in reserve. To their right was Brig. Gen. George Sykes's division of Gouverneur Warren's, Robert Buchanan's, and Charles Lovell's brigades stretching to the road that led to the Grapevine Bridge. In all, Porter had nearly 30,000 men and ample artillery arrayed for the Confederate approach. Lee was in for a nasty surprise.

* * *

A. P. Hill's men advanced, passed Dr. Gaines's mill, and soon arrived at the edge of Boatswain's swamp. This was not on Lee's map, and he had to

On the morning of June 27, Lee, Jackson, and A. P. Hill met at the Walnut Grove Church, which was also used as a field hospital. (aw)

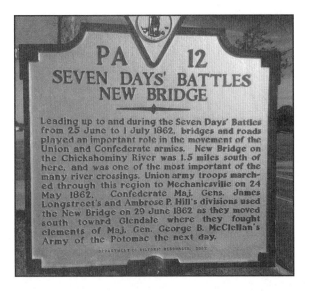

The turn off to New Bridge was a key location for Lee. As his army passed this point, it would once again be able to cross the river to unite with Magruder's and Huger's divisions south of the Chickahominy. (dc)

quickly reevaluate; it was not good ground to attack over. In addition to the swamp, Porter's force was arrayed on a ridge on the other side in three lines. His first line of defense was near the bottom of the ridge, at the edge of the swamp. A second line was mid-way up the ridge, and a third waited at the top—along with the artillery.

The Confederates were on a ridge on the opposite side of the stream. They would have to descend the ridge, cross through the swampy, wooded bottomland and creek, then attack uphill against the three lines of defenders.

It was not a promising sight, but Lee's force had no choice. It had to attack. Lee had staked everything on his strategy north of the Chickahominy and had to follow it through.

Hill's men were on the Cold Harbor Road, and as they were the first to arrive, they would be

A marker to Confederate dead rests in the yard of the Walnut Grove Church. This churchyard is the location of the first battlefield meeting of Robert E. Lee and Stonewall Jackson. (aw)

D. H. Hill and much of Jackson's command would be in the area of Old Cold Harbor Tavern. The 1864 battle would be named for this area. (loc)

the first to attack, intending to strike the Union center in what is today known as "Griffin's Woods." Longstreet was on the river road and would move to A. P. Hill's right. D. H. Hill and Jackson would be farther north, on A. P. Hill's left, near the Old Cold Harbor tavern. At the very least Porter would have to thin his lines in order to stretch to meet the Confederates. At best, D. H. Hill and Jackson would flank Porter, and combined with the remainder of the army, funnel the Federals into the river.

It seemed a good plan, but as was the case on the previous day, success would depend on Jackson's timing in hitting Porter's right.

Once again, Jackson was vexed by unfamiliar terrain. This time, though, he had a guide—a cavalryman who lived in the neighborhood. Jackson instructed the soldier to lead him to Cold Harbor. Little did Jackson know that there were two places with that name, "old" and "new" Cold Harbor. As his troops marched, Jackson could hear the sound of firing growing louder and louder. He asked his guide where the firing was coming from, to which the soldier replied that it was coming from Gaines's Mill. The road for "new" Cold Harbor was taking him in that direction. Jackson quickly stated that he did not want to go to Gaines's Mill; he wanted to go to (old) Cold Harbor, to the left of Gaines's Mill. The guide replied that if Jackson had wanted him to go *there*, he should have said so!

Jackson's men had to double back to get on the correct road, which cost them about an hour and a half, seriously disrupting Lee's timetable for the attack. The lack of good maps was continuing to cost the Confederates dearly.

Thaddeus Lowe, chief aeronaut with the newly formed Union Army Balloon Corps, went aloft in his balloon *Intrepid*, and at about 9:30

According to current-day family members, the back part of this building was the New Cold Harbor Tavern of 1862. (aw)

a.m., reported that the Confederates seemed to be massing for an attack. The message was relayed to McClellan, who was also growing increasingly concerned about his position south of the Chickahominy. In the Richmond defenses, Confederate Gen. John Magruder was busy moving his troops back and forth in order to deceive McClellan that his numbers were larger than they really were, and that he might be preparing to advance—and the ruse was working. Convinced that he was vastly outnumbered, McClellan feared an imminent enemy strike there. Further confirming his fears was a report from Lowe that the Confederates had a balloon of their own aloft south of the river. Why else would it be positioned there, if not preparing for an attack?

At about 2:30 p.m., A. P. Hill ordered his men to advance. As his men moved forward, they came upon the brow of the ridge, then descended towards the swamp and the Union lines on the other side. Federal artillery opened a devastating fire on them. Exploding shells and shrapnel rained

At the Old Cold Harbor intersection, D. H. Hill and Jackson attacked to the right. A. P. Hill would have been behind the photographer. (aw)

Federal troops arrayed in three lines created a formidable position: at the bottom of the hill near the swamp, halfway up the hill, and on the crest. (dc)

down, killing or ghastly wounding men. Hill ordered three batteries to open fire in support, but they had little effect.

Brigadier General Maxcy Gregg's men moved down the ridge to the left where, in places, the underbrush grew thick. In other spots, the creek widened, making it difficult to cross under the storm of enemy fire. Smoke from the gunfire hung low and made vision difficult. The Federals on the other side had built crude earthworks of logs and backpacks, which served to stop some of the Confederate fire. A boy of the 1st South Carolina, 16 years old, carried his regiment's flag and was "shot down three times, twice rising and struggling onward." Another man picked up the flag, but was quickly hit. Still another soldier picked it up, but he "was shot down almost immediately." Despite the horrendous conditions, some of Gregg's men managed to make it across and secure a toe hold on the Federal side.

A. P. Hill's other brigades were not so fortunate. Lawrence O. B. Branch's men, to Gregg's right, attacked bravely, but were driven back only a few yards from Federal line. James Archer's men met the same fate. Dorsey Pender's brigade made some progress, but it, too was beaten back. Attempt after attempt failed to make an impact.

Like the others, Joseph Reid Anderson's men advanced under fire, but neither could they pierce the Union defenses. Charles Field brought his division up in one last attempt, yet they had no more success than had the others.

General Hill's attack lasted several hours, but no one had supported his division. Once again, Jackson had not appeared behind the Federal line. Of the 13,000 men Hill had marched up the Cold Harbor Road that day, more than 2,000 were slaughtered.

Lee's effort to win his first battlefield victory had so far been a failure.

* * *

Jackson's men began reaching Old Cold Harbor, though their line strung out several miles to the rear. Lee worried that the Federals might launch a counterattack against Hill and sent his own aide, Walter Taylor, in search of the tardy general. Taylor first encountered Richard Ewell, and told him to move his forces toward A. P. Hill's. Lee himself soon came upon Ewell and ordered him to attack the center of the enemy's line. He also told Ewell to send couriers to tell the rest of Jackson's command to hurry to the front. A solid soldier, Ewell immediately obeyed.

The first of his men to advance were the Louisiana Tigers, with Maj. Roberdeau Wheat leading them forward. A rifle shot through Wheat's head quickly took him out of the action, and his death soon demoralized the Tigers. Isaac Trimble ordered the 15th Alabama and the 21st Georgia in next, but they, too were beaten back.

Meanwhile, D. H. Hill had arrived at Old Cold Harbor, and his men quickly engaged the Federals of Brig. Gen. George Sykes's U.S. Regular Army troops stationed on that end of the line. At the Confederate right, Longstreet arrived and advanced his men to create a diversion, but he soon thereafter ordered his men to prepare for a full assault.

Even as the battle intensified, for Lee, time was running out. It was now late in the day, with only a few hours of daylight remaining. He had to break the Union line before nightfall, or he feared the Federals would escape across the river.

Jackson finally arrived at Old Cold Harbor. Knowing nothing of the terrain, he was no doubt surprised that Longstreet and A. P. Hill had not driven Porter's corps toward him in full retreat, as Lee had planned. Instead, the battle seemed to be in front of Jackson. Riding to meet Jackson, Lee said, "Ah, General, I am very glad to see you. I had hoped to be with you before." He then added, "That fire is very heavy. Do you think your men can stand it?"

"They can stand almost anything," Jackson replied. "They can stand that!" He rode off to put his army into action.

* * *

Despite their successes at repulsing the Confederate assaults, the Federals were having a rough go of it, too.

Porter ordered reinforcements to help blunt the attacks, and he sent word across the river for support. Henry Slocum sent forward his division from the VI Corps, but it would take some time before these men could arrive at the front. Meanwhile, the Irishmen of the 9th Massachusetts were holding out but running out of ammunition. Soon, the 5th New York Zouaves, in their colorful red uniforms, went in—but suffered severely.

Other units, ordered in, helped stem the Confederate tide, and on the right, George Sykes's men held firm. Porter remembered the Confederates sending wave after wave "in such numbers and so rapidly that it appeared as if their reserves were inexhaustible." For every regiment he could send in, "there seemed to be two or three fresh regiments brought up by the enemy."

Sykes's men fired on the attackers "with two-second fuses, cutting them shorter as the line advanced." Soon the Confederates were almost upon them. "In the head of the charge we gave them canister," and when that was gone, fired "shells without fuses." This was a move born of desperation: the shells could just as easily explode among the defenders.

The noise was so piercing that the "whining of the musket balls that passed over our heads was so loud that when our three-inch rifled cannons were fired they sounded no louder than a firecracker." As Sykes's men ran out of ammunition, they would retire, replenish their supply, and return, only to be hit by more fresh enemy troops. Yet they managed to hold on.

As would become a pattern in this campaign, McClellan left his field commander to fend for himself the best he could. He sent a message to the

V Corps commander in the late afternoon, asking if Porter needed more troops—not that any could arrive before nightfall. He then added, "you must hold your own until dark." Ever convinced that the Confederates outnumbered him, he wrote to Secretary of War Edwin Stanton, "Have a terrible contest. Attacked by greatly superior numbers in all directions on this side . . . we hold our own very nearly." McClellan stated that he "may be forced to give up my position during the night," but if he had "20,000 fresh and good troops we would be sure of a splendid victory to-morrow."

At Gaines's Mill

On land originally saved by the Civil War Trust, the monument to the 11th Mississippi was dedicated in June 2016, making it one of the newest on Richmond's battlefields. (cm)

This area of the battlefield offers an excellent perspective of the Confederate assault. The open expanse of the fields on either side offer a hint of the size of Lee's attack at Gaines's Mill: about 58,000 Confederates, making it four times the size of Pickett's charge at Gettysburg. If you face the

Longstreet advanced across this field—preserved by the Civil War Trust—from the far treeline toward the swamp. All the while, Federals shelled them from in front and from Longstreet's right, across the river. (dc)

Texas monument, then turn to your right, the large field beyond the fence—property saved by the Civil War Trust and now owned by Richmond National Battlefield—is where James Longstreet's men advanced.

The Trust purchased the 285-acre property, known as the "McDougle Tract," in 2012. "The scope of this project completely dwarfs all preservation efforts previously undertaken at Gaines' Mill," Civil War Trust president James Lighthizer said at a 2014 press conference when the Trust turned the land over to the National Park Service. "In just one transaction, we were able to quintuple the amount of land—from 65 acres to 350 acres—protected at the site of Gen. Robert E. Lee's first major victory as commander of the Army of Northern Virginia."

According to the Trust, acquisition of the tract, "with its unique combination of large size, historic pedigree and looming development threat, had long been a priority for preservationists."

Prior to the Trust's purchase of the land, the release explained, "the bulk of protected land at Gaines' Mill was bought in the 1920s by a group of dedicated Richmond residents—including legendary historian and Richmond

News Leader editor Douglas Southall Freeman. This group, the Richmond Battlefield Park Corporation, purchased 60 acres south of Boatswain's Creek that included a portion of the Union line and the Watt House. . . ."

In 1932, the Corporation donated all of its battlefield property, including its Gaines's Mill holdings, to the Commonwealth of Virginia for the creation of a state park. Four years later, the land was transferred to the National Park Service.

However, according to the Trust, "no new land was protected at Gaines's Mill until the second half of the last decade, when the Richmond Battlefields Association saved 3 acres immediately north of the creek, and, in 2011, the Trust bought two more acres further to the east."

Hood's Texas brigade passed through the area where you're now standing, as marked by the Texas monument. Off to the left, the Mississippians advanced. On your way to this tour stop, you passed the monument to the 11th Mississippi, marking their avenue of advance.

The Texas monument, dedicated to John Bell Hood's brigade, which attacked from this area, sits on land acquired by the Richmond Battlefields Association. The monument, made of Texas red granite, resembles the design of Texas state monuments seen at a dozen other battlefields, including Gettysburg and the Wilderness. (aw)

➤ TO STOP 3B:

Return down the dirt road, and turn right on the paved road. This will take you to the Watt house. Pull in to the parking area.

GPS: N 37 57.465, W 77 29.29

Lee's First Victory

CHAPTER SIX

JUNE 27, 1862

Time was running out for Lee. It was now near 7 p.m., and he had at the most an hour or so of daylight left. He had to break the Federal line before the enemy could escape across the river.

Porter felt the desperation of the Confederate attacks trying to drive his men from the field, "evidently a matter of life or death to our opponents' cause." Thick smoke filled the air, making it difficult to see. His ammunition was low, and his men's guns were so fouled by the constant firing that they became difficult to load. The Union commander saw the sun going down and began to hope that his troops could hold out for the remainder of the day and cross the river that night.

Whiting's brigades of Brig. Gen. John Bell Hood and Col. Evander M. Law began arriving, and Lee ordered them to support A. P. Hill's exhausted division on its right. Jackson's command was now divided, with Ewell and Whiting on either side of Hill. On the far right of the Confederate line was Longstreet's division. *Finally* the Confederates were all in position, and now might be their last chance.

Lee was mistakenly convinced that "the principal part of the Federal Army was now on the north side the Chickahominy." Added to this was the fire of the enemy's heavy guns from across the river.

It was now or never. He ordered all of his forces to make one final effort.

It would be his largest attack of the war.

On the far Confederate left, D. H. Hill's men, joined by Ewell's, attacked Sykes's U.S. Regulars

After breaking through the first Federal line of defense, the Texans pushed uphill. The walking trail by the Watt house traces the Texans' footsteps, offering a good idea of just how daunting that uphill assault must have been. Imagine making the climb while under fire, wearing wool in the summer heat, and carrying forty pounds of gear. (cm)

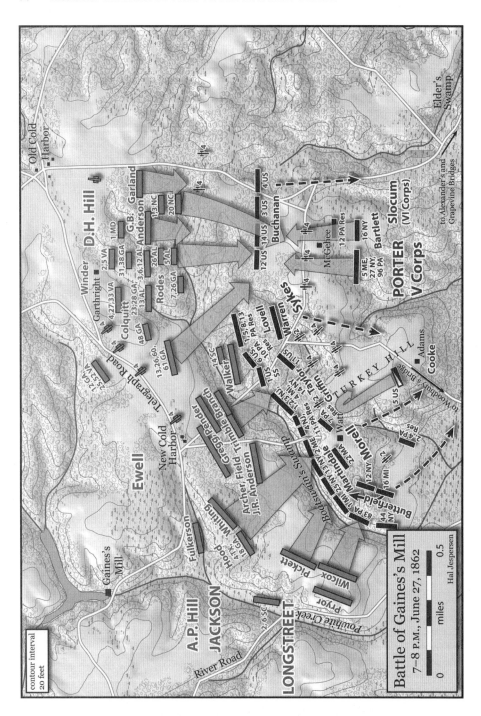

Battle of Gaines's Mill——Lee followed up his initial repulse with the largest Confederate attack of the war to date. This time, the Federal right gave way while Hood's Texas Brigade earned everlasting fame for its strong push through the Federal center. On the Confederate right, Cadmus Wilcox's division took especially high casualties assaulting a strong Federal flank.

Alfred Waud accompanied the Army of the Potomac and created many images of the war. This sketch depicts the action on the Federal left; it also demonstrates that the terrain was much more open than it is today. (loc)

again, but Sykes's troops poured fire into them. On came the Confederates, uttering their "fiendish yell." In the thick smoke, they gathered themselves near the top of the ridge, then made one last assault—this time driving the enemy blue from the crest of the ridge near the McGehee house, turning the farm into a bloody field and capturing some light artillery.

The Federal line was finally pierced.

Longstreet, on the right, also attacked, joined by the men of Law's and Hood's brigades. However, as Longstreet's men advanced across the large field and headed down to the swamp, guns hit them from two directions. On their right, the Federals fired from the south bank of the Chickahominy. At their front, withering Federal artillery fire from the opposite ridge and three lines of infantry down the slope faced Longstreet. The swamp itself, which was wider in this area, added to their misery. The Confederates continued their advance nonetheless.

On Longstreet's immediate left were Hood's and Law's brigades. Lee rode up to Hood and told him that the Union line must be broken—could he do it? Hood replied that he would try. With Hood, that meant his men would make a maximum effort. Lee lifted his hat and said, "May God be with you." A veteran of the 5th Texas wrote, "Gen. Hood dashed to our front, took his hat in his left hand, waived his sword over his head and ordered us to charge."

All Lee could do now was wait.

Hood and Law led their men in the attack. Hood's brigade included the 1st, 4th, and 5th

A National Park Service sign tells the story of the Texas Brigade's breakthrough: the "decisive moment" in the fight. (cm)

Cadmus Wilcox's men attacked the far Federal left at Gaines's Mill and suffered severely—and would do the same three days later at Frayser's Farm/Glendale. Wilcox would rise to division command and would remain active in the Army of Northern Virginia until war's end. (loc)

Texas, the 18th Georgia, and the Hampton Legion. Colonel Law's consisted of the 2nd and 11th Mississippi, 4th Alabama, and the 6th North Carolina. Facing them was George Morell's division, with the brigades of Daniel Butterfield, John Martindale, and Charles Griffin. Ironically, two of Butterfield's regiments—the 44th New York and the 83rd Pennsylvania—would earn fame at Gettysburg a year later helping to hold Little Round Top against Hood's attack there. To the rear, at the top of the hill, was George McCall's brigade, weary from its action on the previous day.

Hood and Law, like Longstreet, took fire as they crossed the open field and descended to the swamp. They pushed through mud and water and, without stopping to fire, overran the first Union works at the bottom of the hill. The defenders fell back, and the Confederates "pushed hard after them," with "Minie Balls whistling all around."

As the Federals retreated, they blocked the vision of the troops higher up, effectively masking the enemy advance. The Confederates thus pushed through the second line, advancing all the way to the top of the hill where they drove off the Federal defenders and captured fourteen pieces of artillery.

The first to pierce the Federal line in that area

According to Lt. Charles A. Phillips of the 5th Massachusetts Battery, the Confederates "rushed through the woods over the brook, now filled with dead bodies, closing their ranks as fast as our fire mowed them down. . . . The woods were full of smoke, and the bullets buzzed round our heads over like a swarm of angry bumblebees. . . . My horse had a bullet in its flank and one sergeant's horse lay dead on the ground." (rnbp)

was the 4th Texas, which suffered mightily for its effort: 570 casualties, including all of its field-grade officers. The combined brigades of Hood and Law would lose 1,018 men that day—a quarter of those who began the assault.

Longstreet's division was attacking to the right. The brigades of Cadmus Wilcox, George Pickett, Roger Pryor, and Winfield Featherston advanced. Richard Anderson's brigade was divided, part of it supporting Pickett and the other guarding the right flank; James Kemper was held in reserve.

Longstreet's men crashed through the swamp and charged up the hill, driving the enemy defenders

Jackson and D. H. Hill advanced against Sykes across this field. (aw)

The Federal right was anchored on this ridge by Sykes's U.S. Army Regulars. At the climax of the battle, Confederates drove them back, but they made an orderly retreat toward the river. (aw)

before them. The entire Federal left now collapsed. Law later recalled that as they fired at the retreating enemy, "scarcely a shot fired into that living mass could fail of its errand." Another similarly remembered the moment: "so terribly horrid is the scene that the imagination could never so far lose all sense of humanity to depict it."

Despite the carnage, victory was within Lee's grasp.

Just then, the unexpected happened, and the Confederates "felt the ground begin to tremble like an earthquake." To Porter's surprise, some of his cavalry attacked in an effort to drive the Confederates back from the guns. Philip St. George Cooke ordered 250 men of the 5th Cavalry, from Porter's reserve, to strike the Confederates at the guns. The days of the cavalry charge against massed infantry had long since passed, and this attack was doomed from the start. All it achieved was the loss of brave troopers and considerable confusion. Porter lost 22 guns that day, and he blamed part of that on the chaos created by the cavalry attack.

Lee's men had finally won the day, but at a terrible cost. He wrote to President Davis that he was "profoundly grateful to Almighty God for the signal victory granted to us," but added, "I grieve to say that our loss in officers and men is great." At the time, Gaines's Mill was the second-bloodiest battle of the war, ranking only behind Shiloh. Roughly 8,700 Confederates and 6,800 Union troops had fallen in the fields that one afternoon.

Mercifully, night was ending the struggle. With daylight nearly gone, the Federals pulled back towards the river. Despite Lee's best efforts, the enemy would escape. He had achieved a victory, but it was not complete, and not enough daylight remained to pursue a more significant triumph.

For years to come, Confederate veterans would argue over who first broke the Federal line. Was it Hood's 4th Texans or was it D. H. Hill's men, who had driven back George Sykes's regulars on the Union right? No one would ever be sure, but in the end, it wasn't important except to the men in the units who had a stake in the argument. What actually mattered was that Confederates had shattered George McClellan's position north

Several years after the battle, exposed remains littered the Gaines's Mill battlefield. (loc)

of the Chickahominy. The Federal commander would now do everything possible to race towards the safety of the James River, where he planned to establish a new base.

If he were to fail, it would mean disaster. For both sides, the stakes could not be higher. Time was the enemy of both.

At the Watt House

In the 1860s, the Watt house farm was known as "Springfield Plantation." Today, it's a private residence. (cm)

Known as "Springfield" during the war, the Watt house is thought to have been built around 1836 by Hugh Watt and his wife Sarah (Sarah Bohannon Kidd). George Watt, their son, invented the Watt plow. Two daughters married Haw brothers, one of whom lived at Haw's Shop, the site of the 1864 battle of that name.

The fighting devastated the Watt farm, but miraculously the house survived. After a succession of owners, it was ultimately sold to the Richmond National Battlefield Park (RNBP). During the 1930s, the Civilian Conservation Corps repaired the building, and over the years, RNBP has continued to restore it. Today, the home appears to be in nearly perfect condition, and members of the RNBP staff live in it. As it is a private residence, please respect the privacy of those who live here. You are free to walk the grounds, although other outbuildings have long disappeared.

Down the hill, in front of the parking area, a trail through the woods follows the Confederate path used to attack the Union lines. Walking this route is the best way to understand the battle. Be sure to take the extended path. Markers show where

A pair of 12–pound Napoleons stand near the Watt house, marking the Federals' third line of defense. (dc)

Hood's breakthrough occurred, and there is a monument to Wilcox's brigade. The battlefield extended two miles to the east from your current position, crossing farmland. Be aware that the farm is private property.

If you take the trail, winding through the woods and down to the creek, you will approach from the Union perspective to where the Confederates crossed. The ground was a bit more open in 1862 as this was a farm and animals ate much of the smaller vegetation. Large trees grew, however, so it was not completely clear.

As you stand at the creek, turn around and look up the hill. Imagine three rows of Union defenders lined across it. One line set up near where you were standing, one midway up, and one near the top. This is one of the Civil War's most poignant views. The Union defensive position was very strong. Imagine being a Confederate soldier, charging down the opposite hill, crossing the creek, and facing this defensive line. Also, put yourself in the place of a Northern soldier, trying to hold your ground against that onslaught.

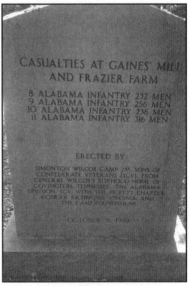

Wilcox's men suffered severely at Gaines's Mill and would do the same three days later at Frazier's Farm/Glendale. Their high casualties reflect the cost of Lee's first victory. (dc)

Side Stop: Cold Harbor

The National Park Service's Cold Harbor Visitor Center offers orientation about the campaigns of 1862 and 1864, both of which spilled across this landscape. The 1862 battle of Gaines's Mill and the 1864 battle of Cold Harbor were fought on much of the same ground but perpendicular to each other. (cm)

You have the option to extend your tour to a side stop—one highly recommended. As you leave Gaines's Mill, turn right. In a short distance, you will see the Cold Harbor Battlefield Park on your left. Also, this site provides restrooms. A knowledgeable ranger is always on duty, and an electronic map describes the battles of Gaines's Mill and Cold Harbor.

The Cold Harbor and Gaines's Mill battlefields, which occupy some of the same ground, sit perpendicular to each other. A walk through the wooded trails will give you an excellent idea of how the fields of battle in 1864 differed from those of 1862—in 1864, troops made much greater use of entrenchments. Cold Harbor has some of the best-preserved earthworks in America.

➤ TO STOP 4: Savage's Station

After crossing the Chickahominy River, tour-followers will pass a commuter lot on the right. There, a state historical plaque and a Freeman monument mark the story of Grapevine Bridge. However, aside from being rich in Civil War history, this area is also rich with ecological diversity. A nature preserve gives visitors the opportunity to explore the banks of the swampy river. (cm)

Turn left out of the Cold Harbor parking lot.

In about one mile from the Cold Harbor visitor center, you will come to an intersection. The Old Cold Harbor tavern would have been directly in front of you, but it no longer stands. Turn right onto the cross street.

(Note: As you turn, be aware that the Confederates used the road you have been on, from the Watt House all the way to the to this corner, as the base for their attacks at Gaines's Mill. D. H. Hill and Jackson arrived at the intersection. When you turn right, you will be following the direction of their attack.) Drive 3.6 miles to the next turn.

Many interpretive signs stand along this route. Please exercise great care if you decide to pull off to read them— this can be a busy road!

In about a half a mile, you will reach a ridge with a sign that discusses Sykes's defense. This was the far right of the Union position. Farther on, you will come to another ridge. If you glance to your right you will see a farm. This is Turkey Hill, the main defensive position of the Union army; it stretches back to the Watt House.

A Civil War Trails marker in the front yard of the Trent House shows an earlier scene from the yard: Federal aeronauts once more took to the air to do reconnaissance. (cwt/vhs)

Interestingly, it was also the Confederate right flank during the battle of Cold Harbor two years later. Please note that it is private property.

Continue on the same road. You will pass a convenience store on your right. Beyond the store, you will cross a bridge; this is the area of the Grapevine Bridge. When the road becomes four lanes, immediately get in your

From the yard of the Trent house, Federal aeronauts once more took to the air to do reconnaissance. (vhs)

The Trent house served as the headquarters of General McClellan. In 1862, the road ran on the other side of the house. Today, this is private property. (aw)

left lane. Make the first left turn onto Old Hanover Road. Almost immediately there will be another left, marked by a Richmond Battlefield tour route sign. Turn left onto Grapevine Road.

Down the road a short distance, you will see on the right an old house, as well as a Civil War Trails marker. This is the Trent house, the headquarters of George McClellan. At the time of the war, the road ran on the other side of the house. Please respect that the house is private property.

Continue down Grapevine Road until it ends and turn left. Once you have turned, the Savage's Station battlefield will be on your right. You will see a group of markers where you can pull off. Sadly, the property is not accessible—nothing remains of the battlefield except farmland and a major highway intersection.

Remained parked for the next three chapters

GPS: N 37 52.879, W 77 27.032

Savage's Station

CHAPTER SEVEN

JUNE 28-29, 1862

At first light on June 28, dead and wounded lay all about, while the cries and moans of the latter filled the morning air. Confederate soldier Thomas Penn wrote to his mother: "I am seated under a tree right upon the battle ground which is strewn with the dead and dying. Their groans are constantly heard upon every side." This would become an all-too-familiar sight for the men in both armies.

As Lee surveyed the scene, he could see that the enemy had abandoned the north side of the Chickahominy. As the Federals retreated, they also had destroyed all of the bridges east of New Bridge. There was no simple way to get at them.

What was McClellan planning to do? With the bridges out, it was unlikely he would cross back over the river to attack. Staying where he was would be difficult, though, as Stuart reported that the Federals were burning their supply base at White House and had lost the use of the railroad. Keeping the army supplied would prove a challenge. This, plus McClellan's obviously cautious nature, made an attack directly at Richmond improbable.

Two options remained. First, the Federal army could retreat down the Peninsula, perhaps to reorganize and move on Richmond again. To watch for this threat, Lee sent Stuart and his troopers east to keep an eye out for a move in that direction. Stuart was joined by the division of Richard Ewell.

The second option seemed more likely: a Federal move south to the James River, where they could set up a new base of operations under the

Sadly, all that remains of the Savage's Station battlefield is a Civil War Trails pull-off and an array of signs. (cm)

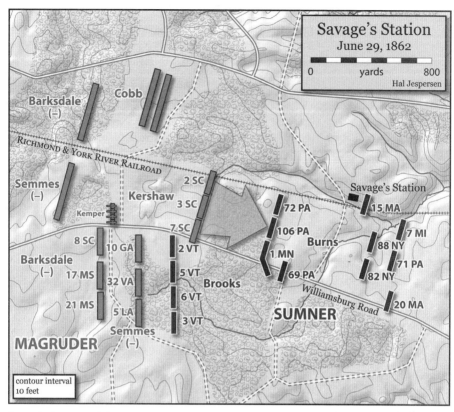

SAVAGE'S STATION—With the Williamsburg Road and Richmond and York River Railroad creating an alley of attack, Kershaw's South Carolinians went straight at Sumner's middle, outflanking his brigade of Vermonters entirely. Federals held until day's end, however, before safely withdrawing.

protection of their gunboats. This, too, would be difficult for McClellan. Few good roads ran south, and he had an army of 100,000 men, 281 field guns, 26 heavy guns, 3,800 wagons, and 2,500 head of cattle. It was a logistical nightmare—but it was the strategy McClellan ultimately chose.

The day wore on. With Stuart and Ewell reporting no serious activity in their area, Lee determined that McClellan was indeed heading for the James, and he drew up a plan to catch the Federal army on the move and seriously injure, if not destroy, it. Lee had a good network of roads to work with. North to south, he had the Williamsburg, Charles City, and Darbytown roads. At the river was the aptly named River Road. Near New Market, the River Road split off the Long Bridge Road, which ran northeast and touched Darbytown, leading to an intersection with Charles City and Willis Church

Roads, known locally as "Riddell's Shop" (now referred to as "Glendale"). From that intersection a road ran down to Malvern Hill, a gentle, sloping eminence that would dominate any attempt to reach the James.

Lee saw a great opportunity. The part of his army south of the Chickahominy, under Maj. Gen. John B. Magruder and Maj. Gen. Benjamin Huger, would temporarily stay put, just in case McClellan turned toward Richmond. Longstreet and A. P. Hill would cross at New Bridge and head for the Darbytown Road. Jackson could rebuild bridges destroyed by the retreating Federals and follow them. Major General Theophilus H. Holmes would be called up from the Petersburg area and head east along the River Road.

Once Lee's spread-out command was ready, Magruder and Huger would strike the retreating Federal column, holding it in place, and then A. P. Hill and Longstreet would attack at Riddell's Shop, cutting the Federals in two. Holmes, from the River Road, could possibly strike the head of the enemy column. Jackson would come down from the north, cross the river, and deliver a smashing sledgehammer blow. If all went well, part, if not most, of the Federal army might be destroyed.

It was a bold, if complicated, plan. Lee had a group of leaders he did not yet know. Maps were poor. Time would tell if his generals could pull off his plan. However, one thing was certain: he was proving true Joseph Ives's prediction that Lee would be audacious.

Known as "Prince John," John Bankhead Magruder earned his nickname for his sense of flourish in his wardrobe and his sense of theatrics on the battlefield. Magruder turned in a command performance during the spring, but the Seven Days' would be an inglorious curtain call for him in the Eastern Theatre. (loc)

* * *

On June 29, Magruder met Lee on the Nine Mile Road. Magruder was under the impression that Huger would move down the Williamsburg Road in support and Jackson would cross the Chickahominy. Some 35,000 to 40,000 Confederates would strike and crush the rear of the Federal retreat. The opportunity seemed excellent.

Unfortunately for Magruder, things began unraveling immediately. Jackson would not cross the Chickahominy. The retreating Federals had destroyed the bridges in his area, and they needed rebuilding, a time-consuming process that Jackson did not hurry.

First, he ordered Maj. Robert L. Dabney, a preacher before the war, to repair the bridges, but Dabney was ill prepared for the task. Jackson then

The train depot that gave Savage's Station its name gave the area strategic importance. (loc)

sent for Capt. C. R. Mason, an engineer, but Mason was 15 miles away.

According to Jackson's biographer, Dr. James Robertson, there was an additional reason for Stonewall's delay: Jackson was obeying orders. In a message to Jeb Stuart, Col. R. H. Chilton, Lee's assistant adjutant general, stated, "The Gen'l Comd'g requests that you will watch the Chicahominy [sic] as far as Forge Bridge, ascertain if any attempt will be made in that direction by the enemy, advising Genl Jackson, who will resist their passage until reinforced."

When Magruder sent an officer to inquire as to when Jackson would come to Magruder's aid, he received the reply that the Valley commander had "other important duty to perform."

As they began advancing, Magruder's men could see smoke in the distance from the direction of Savage's Station. The Federals were on the move, destroying everything they couldn't carry away. They burned mountains of beef, hardtack, coffee, rifles and other supplies. They set an ammunition train ablaze. Also, 2,500 to 3,500 sick and wounded men too ill to move were left to the mercy of the enemy.

In order to protect his rear, McClellan ordered the corps of Edwin Sumner, William Franklin, and Samuel Heintzelman to take up positions near Savage's Station. He then departed, not to return, and unfortunately for his soldiers, he left no one in overall command.

Sumner set up in advance of the others at Allen's

An ordnance train explodes in the background as Federals try to retreat after the battle. (loc)

Farm; consequently, the three corps did not present a contiguous front. Franklin established a position further south, up between the railroad and the Williamsburg Road, fully expecting Heintzelman to be positioned nearby. To his dismay, this did not occur—a result of McClellan having not appointed a commander.

Magruder's advancing force ran into Sumner at Allen's, and, after a brief fight, drove them back. As Magruder looked for Jackson to cross the Chickahominy, he wondered where his support to the right was. Huger, who had been ordered to send two brigades to assist Magruder, was not moving down the Williamsburg Road as Magruder had expected.

Fearing that he might be attacked, and waiting for Jackson, Magruder hesitated for a few hours, during which time, Huger's brigades were recalled. That left Magruder to attack an enemy of unknown size with only his own command.

Regardless, his orders remained: he was to attack.

Lafayette McLaws's division approached the station first, with Joseph Kershaw sending a regiment to "ascertain the conditions of things in the front." They received some artillery fire on their left flank, but did not immediately return it, fearing that it might be Jackson's men coming down from the Chickahominy. In order to signal Jackson that he was firing on friends, Kershaw ordered a regimental flag waived—which soon made it apparent that the fire was not from Jackson, but from the Federals. Union generals Franklin and John Sedgwick rode out, expecting to find Heintzelman, and indeed saw troops in the distance, but upon closer inspection Sedgwick exclaimed, "Why, those men are Rebels!"

Around 3 p.m., Kershaw received orders to advance, and he soon saw Federal troops occupying earthworks in the distance. He directed Del Kemper's battery up in support. The colonel of the 7th South Carolina, D. Wyatt Aiken, ordered his men to advance and fire at will. As they did, Kemper's guns "inflicted terrible havoc upon the enemy, whose dead lay in heaps along the road, scarcely 200 yards" from the battery.

Federal Brig. Gen. William Burns held the woods between the railroad and Williamsburg Road with two regiments, the 72nd and 106th Pennsylvania. With Kershaw's South Carolina troops fast approaching, Burns sent an urgent call for reinforcements, and quickly the 1st Minnesota appeared on the left. Kershaw's men began to break through, but Burns's men rallied and held. The 88th New York came rushing up at the double-quick, joined by the 82nd New York. The 69th Pennsylvania was placed on the far left. Other units soon joined them. The Federals held—in this area.

General Lafayette McLaws sent Paul Semmes's brigade south of the Williamsburg Road. The woods were thick, but Semmes's men were able to make out some troops in the distance. Semmes ordered Private Maddox of the 5th Louisiana to challenge: "What regiment?"

"Third Vermont!" came the prompt response. The Confederates opened fire on them.

The action lasted until darkness covered the field. William Brooks, commander of the William Smith's 2nd Brigade, had four Vermont regiments stationed south of the road—the 2nd, 3rd, 5th and 6th. Facing them were Semmes's men of the 10th Georgia, 32nd Virginia, and the 5th Louisiana.

Magruder sent Col. William Barksdale across the road in support of Semmes. The men from Vermont fought fiercely, many using all of the 60 rounds of ammunition they had been allotted. The 5th Vermont then exploded into a bayonet charge, "which was executed at a double-quick in splendid style."

Despite the heroics on both sides, neither gained an advantage, and darkness soon descended upon the field.

Strategically, the Federals had the best of the

Part of the battle took place on this farmland; another part of the battlefield is buried beneath modern highways. (dc)

day. They had blunted the Confederate attack, held their position, and kept the Federal rear safe for the moment.

Sumner was soon surprised to learn that he did not have the three corps he had expected. Heintzelman, following his own whim, had decided there were too many troops in the area, so he moved his out, in the direction of White Oak Swamp. Regardless, the Federals had more than enough troops to do the job. With the failure of Jackson to cross the Chickahominy and the lack of support from Huger, Magruder only had his own 13,000 men on hand. To compound this shortfall, he only sent in part of his command.

Lee was growing increasingly frustrated that his plans were not being carried out and that the Federals were thus allowed to escape. "I regret much that you have made so little progress today in the pursuit of the enemy," he wrote sharply to Magruder. "In order to reap the fruits of our victory the pursuit should be more vigorous. I urge you, then, to press on his rear rapidly and steadily."

As disappointed as Lee was, one cannot attribute all of the blame to Magruder. Jackson and Huger had failed to coordinate, and Lee had not sent staff officers to ensure their compliance with his orders. It was a new army, and it was feeling its growing pains.

Unfortunately for Lee, the issue would reappear as the week wore on.

W 13

ROUTE TO WHITE OAK SWAMP AND MALVERN HILL

After crossing the Chickahominy River to the north of Grapevine Bridge, portions of Maj. Gen. George B. McClellan's retreating Union army destroyed the bridge and moved southeast along this road on 28 June 1862. After rebuilding the bridge the next day, Maj. Gen. Thomas J. ("Stonewall") Jackson's command (which included his own division and those of Generals Richard S. Ewell, William H. C. Whiting, and Daniel H. Hill) began crossing early in the morning of 30 June. Under orders to clear the enemy from the woods south of the Chickahominy and to follow McClellan's retreating army, Jackson's men captured numerous prisoners as they advanced along this road.

The Race is On

CHAPTER EIGHT

JUNE 28-30, 1862

That night, the Federals at Savage's Station received word that McClellan expected all of the troops to be across White Oak Swamp by the next morning. They dutifully pulled out at 1 a.m., enduring a bone-wearying march, with men dropping and falling asleep by the roadside only to be awakened by the cavalry bringing up the rear, riders who warned foot soldiers that they would be certain prisoners if they did not get up and move.

The exhausted infantry was strung out as it arrived near the White Oak crossing. General Israel Richardson, "swearing like a trooper," waited for them to cross so he could burn the bridge.

Captain George Hazzard and his battery almost didn't make it. They were deep in sleep as the army pulled out. In the morning, Hazzard awoke to reveille—but it was coming from the wrong direction! The men hastily arose and headed for the bridge, arriving just before Richardson set fire to it. Despite this close escape, the day would prove to be very bad for Hazzard: he would be mortally wounded a few hours later.

McClellan established a strong defensive position to protect his army during the remainder of its retreat. He protected his rear at White Oak Swamp with Richardson's division of the II Corps, Smith's division of the VI Corps, Naglee's brigade of the IV Corps, and three artillery batteries—all situated high on a ridge overlooking White Oak. From their position, the

As McClellan continued to try to slip away, Confederates continued to nip at his heels. Federals effectively staved off Confederates, although the army trickled a steady stream of men who fell prisoner. (cm)

One of Jackson's finest subordinates, Richard Ewell fought near Old Cold Harbor. A year later, he would be in command of Jackson's corps. (loc)

hill descended to the swamp, which was nearly as impassable as the Chickahominy. After a stretch of bottomland, it rose again on the other side, where the Confederates would soon arrive. On that far side grew woods, which would provide good cover for the enemy's artillery.

The road from the Federal position at White Oak ran southwest about two miles to the intersection at Riddell's Shop. To the west of the crossroads, along Charles City Road, Henry Slocum's division of the VI Corps guarded McClellan's flank. Farther to the south, about a mile west of the intersection, were George McCall's men of the V Corps. Having been bloodied at Beaver Dam Creek and again at Gaines's Mill, these troops should have been placed in the rear for rest. Instead, they ended up at the front facing the brunt of the Confederate attack later that day.

To McCall's left, near the Willis Church, was Joseph Hooker's division of the III Corps. John Sedgwick's division of the II Corps was posted to the rear near the Nelson house, which set on a farm once owned by the Frayser family. The locals still often referred to the area as the "Frayser's Farm," and owing to the events that would occur later that day, it would be forever known by that name. About a mile south from Hooker was Malvern Hill.

Not an impressive eminence, Malvern nonetheless provided a perfect setting for artillery. An open space of about 900 yards across, with a gentle slope, it offered a nearly perfect field of fire. Porter's V Corps with the army's artillery reserve had stopped there after its retreat from Gaines's Mill.

The remainder of Erasmus Keyes's IV Corps was stationed close to the James River. McClellan's army was thus strung out, with many units positioned away from their respective corps. The defense also lacked continuity, with several breaks in the line. To make matters even worse, McClellan rode off toward the river looking for a strong position for his new base. Once again, he left no one in overall command. As on the previous day, his subordinates would have to fend for themselves.

The Federals destroyed their supply base on the Pamunkey as they abandoned it. The chimneys are the remains of Rooney Lee's home; George Washington had once courted Martha Custis there. (loc)

* * *

Stonewall Jackson finally crossed the Chickahominy and arrived at Magruder's camp around 3:30 on the morning of June 30. As the sun rose, the evidence of McClellan's hurried retreat was everywhere: mountains of beef, grain, medicine, knapsacks, blankets, and other implements. He'd also left behind 2,500 sick and wounded Federal troops. Added to this were about 1,000 stragglers, and of course, the Union dead from the previous day's battle. Horrifying piles of amputated arms and legs were strewn about. "I discovered what appeared to be a line of battle drawn up at the station, but which proved to be a line of sick and of hospital attendants," D. H. Hill recalled. He then saw "what seemed to be an entire regiment of Federals cold in death, and learned that a Vermont regiment [the 5th] had been in the desperate charge upon the division of McLaws." It was an overwhelming sight.

The Union army's detritus and left-behinds signaled to the Confederates a need for haste: McClellan was escaping. Lee's frustration was growing, but there was still a chance to damage or destroy a large part of the Federal army.

Ewell's division had returned from its assignment to keep an eye for a retreat by the enemy down the peninsula. A. P. Hill and Longstreet had crossed over the Chickahominy and had camped for the night at Jacob Atlee's farm (now Dorey Park) on the Darbytown Road. Benjamin Huger's division had not accomplished much, but it was positioned on the Charles City

When the Federals marched to the James River, the army left behind many of its wounded at a field hospital at Savage's Station. (loc)

Road, in direct line to the Glendale crossroads. Theophilus Holmes had been ordered to cross the James and was marching up the River Road. Jackson's men were heading for White Oak Swamp, while Magruder rested for an hour—his first sleep in 48. Lee's army was nearly in position with about 70,000 men.

With so much riding on the day's action, Lee rode to meet Jackson. The artillerist Robert Stiles recalled Lee's arrival, saying that the commanding general was immaculately attired when he dismounted gracefully from his horse. On the other hand, Jackson "appeared worn down to the lowest point of flesh consistent with effective service." His clothes were "one neutral dust tint."

Greeting each other warmly, the two generals got right to business. Stiles saw Jackson talk in "a jerky, impetuous way" and drew a diagram in the dust with his boot. He traced two lines and, as he drew the third, exclaimed, "We've got him!" Jackson immediately mounted his horse and rode away.

The two leaders seemed to be in complete agreement. Would the day turn out as planned?

Federal guns waited in position near Gouldin's farm, also known as "Golding's farm." (loc)

Would they be able to strike a potentially fatal blow to the enemy's largest army?

Down by the River

CHAPTER NINE

JUNE 30, 1862

Thus far, Benjamin Huger had done little of consequence. Following Lee's orders, his division had remained south of the Chickahominy while most of the rest of the army had attacked farther north. He had been of no assistance to Magruder but instead had marched down the Charles City Road.

June 30 was his opportunity.

Because he was south of White Oak Swamp and thus the closest to the Glendale intersection, he would strike first. His attack would lend great weight to Longstreet and A. P. Hill, who would advance on his right. He formed the hinge between those two commanders and Jackson. The prospects of the day looked great, but it would require aggressive movement.

On this morning, Huger gave orders to Ambrose Wright to recross the White Oak Swamp and search for Phil Kearny's men, whom Huger thought might be on their flank. However, Kearny had retreated back down the swamp, leaving a few troops behind to guard his retreat. William Mahone's men were in the Confederate lead, and south of the swamp they soon ran into the Federal rear guard, which had been cutting down trees to block the Confederates' progress.

Rather than send troops ahead to stop the Federals from chopping trees, Mahone instead plugged away at removing obstructions. He then decided his best course of action would be to cut a new road—a disastrous decision that halted the progress of Huger's column.

About two miles northwest of Glendale, Mahone ordered a battery up to fire on the Federals

New Market Heights offered a position of great natural strength, although now, little remains in the area to suggest its wartime importance. (dd)

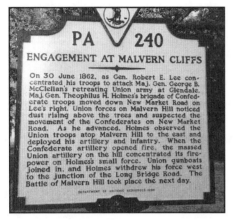

PA ▽ 240

ENGAGEMENT AT MALVERN CLIFFS

On 30 June 1862, as Gen. Robert E. Lee concentrated his troops to attack Maj. Gen. George B. McClellan's retreating Union army at Glendale, Maj. Gen. Theophilus H. Holmes's brigade of Confederate troops moved down New Market Road on Lee's right. Union forces on Malvern Hill noticed dust rising above the trees and suspected the movement of the Confederates on New Market Road. As he advanced, Holmes observed the Union troops atop Malvern Hill to the east and deployed his artillery and infantry. When the Confederate artillery opened fire, the massed Union artillery on the hill concentrated its firepower on Holmes's small force. Union gunboats joined in, and Holmes withdrew his force west to the junction of the Long Bridge Road. The Battle of Malvern Hill took place the next day.

DEPARTMENT OF HISTORIC RESOURCES 1994

A state historic marker describes Theophilus Holmes's futile attack on the Federal left on June 30. (dc)

in the distance. This marked the extent of Huger's progress on June 30. Not only would Lee lose the services of an entire division in the center of his attack, but Huger's inactivity would also give the Federals to his front the opportunity to send reinforcements to another sector of the battle at a key moment. Lee would not forget Huger's performance this day.

Huger was not alone in his failings, however.

* * *

Down on the River Road, Theophilus Holmes was advancing toward Malvern Hill. If he could arrive there before the Federals, he might even be able to seize the hill and cut off their retreat. Combined with the attacks of A. P. Hill, Longstreet, Huger, and Jackson, the Confederates would have the enemy in a vise.

By 10 a.m., Holmes's force reached the heights at New Market, "a position of great natural strength," which covered the intersection of the River and Long Bridge Roads. It was an excellent place to protect the Confederate right flank. President Davis, riding out from Richmond to check on the army's progress, rode up to Holmes, and even he approved of the position.

However, protecting the flank was not all that Holmes could do there. A short distance ahead was Malvern Hill. Colonel Tom Rosser of the 5th Virginia Cavalry sent pickets ahead, and they reported that Federal troops were hurriedly moving into position on the hill. He rode to tell Holmes, but "no attention was paid to this report." Frustrated, Rosser then sent word to Lee, who came down himself to view the situation, and he promptly ordered an attack. Despite Lee's orders and the urgency of the situation, Holmes seemed to be in no great hurry. It took him until 5 p.m. to prepare his assault.

On the Union side, Porter was wasting no time creating a strong position on Malvern, assembled of two divisions of his V Corps plus eight batteries of artillery. George Sykes's men topped the hill, and Gouverneur Warren's troops waited in the valley to the south.

The Confederate major general sent six guns ahead to "greatly embarrass" the Federals. Unfortunately for the Confederates, the embarrassment belonged not to Porter's troops.

V V 5
TURKEY ISLAND

Soon after landing at Jamestown in May 1607, Captain Christopher Newport, while exploring the James River discovered Turkey Island (two miles south). He named it for the large number of wild turkeys there. In 1684, William Randolph purchased Turkey Island; it then became the seat of the Randolph family. His descendants included Thomas Jefferson, John Marshall, and Robert E. Lee. Robert Pickett acquired Turkey Island in 1836. During the Civil War, the large family dwelling was burned by Union troops. Maj. Gen. George E. Pickett and his family lived there in a small cottage after the war.

Holmes's men began to move forward and soon felt the shelling of the heavy 9- and 11-inch Dahlgren guns and 100-pound Parrotts of the *Galena* and the *Aroostook* of the Federal river fleet. The effect was "appalling" as the shells exploded among the men and in the treetops, causing great limbs to come crashing down on them. Then the Federal cannon on Malvern joined the barrage.

In the area of Turkey Island, Holmes's men were pushed back by Federal artillery. (dc)

In a rare moment of humor, Holmes went into a house, and being quite deaf, emerged to say, "I thought I heard firing!"

However, Holmes's attack was falling apart. Warren's men tore into them with infantry fire, stopping the attackers completely. Holmes achieved nothing of consequence this day.

It is uncertain whether Holmes could have moved Porter off the hill with a more prompt attack—the answer will never be known. The Federals held, and the Confederates would feel the consequence of this just a few days later.

As badly as that attack went, it triggered other events of worse tactical impact. Having received word that Holmes needed assistance, Longstreet ordered Magruder to march his 13,000 men down to the river to Holmes's aid. Although Magruder's men would arrive too late to help Holmes, their movement took them out of position to support Longstreet and A. P. Hill—an action with serious repercussions later in the day.

Side Stop: Fort Harrison

Much of the action in this chapter takes place near an area called New Market Heights. Geographically and sequentially, it is too difficult to include the area on the driving tour, although an optional visit after the tour concludes is

Holmes was positioned in this area before his abortive effort towards Malvern Cliffs. New Market Heights was also the site of a noteworthy battle in 1864. (dc)

within relatively easy striking range. Directions can be found at the end of Chapter Thirteen.

There is little to see at New Market Heights itself aside from a state historical marker, alongside the road, which refers to the 1864 battle. That battle was part of a larger effort against Fort Harrison. On September 29, 1964, Gen. Benjamin Butler, commanding the Army of the James, launched a two-pronged attack at the Confederate lines north of the James River. The goal was to break the lines with a surprise attack of overwhelming force in order to surprise and capture Richmond.

Butler made one of the thrusts across the James River at Deep Bottom, near the sight of two failed Federal efforts (First and Second Deep Bottom). This attack achieved much different results. Brigadier General Charles Paine's division of United States Colored Troops (USCT) spearheaded the assault, which succeeded, finally breaking the Confederate position at New Market Heights. Fourteen of the USCT would be awarded the Medal of Honor for their actions.

The left wing of Butler's attack was made at Fort Harrison. While the Federals seized this key position, they were unable to take advantage of their success and failed to break through toward Richmond.

The National Park Service has several sites in this area, including Forts Harrison, Gilmer, and Hoke. Forts Johnson and Gregg are also on the tour route. However, no portion of the New Market Heights battlefield has been preserved. During the summer months the park operates a small visitor center at Fort Harrison.

▶TO STOP 5: WHITE OAK

The next phase of the tour—the ten-mile stretch between Savage's Station and White Oak Swamp—will feel like a relatively long haul. Turn right out of the Savage's Station pull-off. In about two miles, you will come to a stop sign, after which you will continue straight. In a few more miles, you will come to a traffic light. Continue straight at that

RIGHT: Benjamin Huger did not perform well during the campaign, and his subsequent days with the Army of Northern Virginia would be short lived. (loc)

LEFT: Henry W. Slocum fought at First Manassas, where he was wounded, then returned to lead troops on the Peninsula and through the Seven Days. (loc)

Huger's lack of activity allowed Henry Slocum to send Federal reinforcements to the heavily engaged Phil Kearny at a crucial moment. (loc)

intersection. You will cross Interstate 64, then Route 60 and, near it, the historic Williamsburg Road. The old road is about one hundred yards past the modern Williamsburg Road. It is the route Cornwallis took from Richmond to Williamsburg during the Revolutionary War.

In a little over three miles, you will come to a pull-off with a Civil War Trails marker. Stop beside the marker.

GPS: N 37 46.997, W 77 21.063

White Oak: Where is Jackson?

CHAPTER TEN

JUNE 30, 1862

On the morning of the 30th, Major General Jackson's men continued past Savage's Station in pursuit of the retreating Federals. Around noon, Stonewall's cavalry reached White Oak Swamp, a nearly impassable morass of muck, vines, and trees. The small stream would swell after rains, and the spongy bottomland around it made it nearly impossible to move men or heavy equipment through without a bridge. On either side were hills, "descended by gentle declivities on both sides."

As Jackson approached the swamp, he found that Federals had destroyed the bridge as well as another one a short distance away at Brackett's Ford. The terrain on Jackson's side was open on his right, with a forest of pines to his left. Across the swamp, the hill was open land, which soon turned to woods. A tall belt of timber ran along the edge of the stream itself, screening the Federals from Jackson's view.

Jackson ordered his 26-year-old chief of artillery, Col. Stapleton Crutchfield, to find a location where he could mass his guns. Crutchfield—who would lose a leg at Chancellorsville in 1863 and be killed at Sailor's Creek in 1865—took advantage of the clear area to the right. As he opened fire, the Federals across the swamp returned it, but soon were driven back, at which point they established another position about 1,000 yards from the Confederate guns.

Although firing continued "without intermission" throughout the day, the effect on either side was

Withoutt the utility lines, White Oak Swamp today would look just as it did in 1862. (cm)

Alfred Waud sketched this view of White Oak artillery in action. (loc)

slight. The sound of the bombardment alarmed John Sedgwick, who was stationed at the Nelson Farm at Glendale. He ordered two of his brigades, those under Brig. Gen. Napoleon J. T. Dana and Brig. Gen. Willis A. Gorman, to march the two miles to White Oak to offer support.

Federal Maj. Gen. William "Baldy" Smith remembered that when the Confederates opened fire, they were "throwing an immense quantity of iron—in fact the air seemed literally full of it." He searched for his horse, but the groom "had taken my best horse in the direction of safety, and I saw no more of him or horse for two days."

General Franklin recalled an encounter with a local farmer who was going to take this wife and children to safety and then return. Puzzled, Franklin asked why he would come back. "Why, if I don't, your men will take all my chickens and ducks!" the farmer replied. Later, after the farmer returned, a piece of shrapnel struck him and took off his leg. He quickly bled to death. Franklin sadly commented, "He had sacrificed himself for his poultry."

In an effort to determine the strength of the enemy position on the other side of the swamp, Jackson and D. H. Hill accompanied Thomas Munford's 2nd Virginia Cavalry as it attempted to cross. As they plunged in, their horses floundered, belly-deep in muck and mire. The Federals began to rain fire down on them, forcing Jackson's party to turn back. "[F]ast riding in the wrong direction is not military," Hill later admitted, "but it is sometimes healthy."

The Union position was much too strong to attack, so Jackson ordered Munford to search for

Similar to the Chickahominy, the waters of White Oak Swamp could rise dramatically after a heavy rain. Steep banks rose on either side. (loc)

another crossing point. The cavalier soon located an undefended cow path where he thought Jackson's infantry could cross. "I had seen his infantry cross in far worse places," Munford recalled, "and I expected that he would attempt it."

Wade Hampton found another promising location about a quarter of a mile away. The swamp there was very narrow—about 10 to 15 feet across—and the bottom was sandy, good for crossing. The Federals there were inattentive, lying down, and relaxing. The Confederate general returned to Jackson and said he could build a bridge there, which Jackson instructed him to do.

After completing the construction, General Hampton returned to his commander to report that the bridge was ready. Jackson merely rose and walked off in silence. Stunned, Hampton returned to his troops.

Yet another crossing point also showed promise: the aforementioned Brackett's Ford, a short distance away. Although Federals had destroyed the bridge, General Franklin still considered it passable, and the Union general later said that Jackson "ought to have known" of the ford and "ought to have discovered the weakness of our defense at that point." Franklin believed that had Jackson attacked there, he would have "embarrassed us exceedingly."

When Hampton departed, Stonewall Jackson sat down and fell asleep. He arose for dinner with his staff, and then once again fell asleep. Later he arose abruptly and said, "[N]ow gentlemen, let us at once to bed and rise at dawn, and see if tomorrow we cannot do something!"

In retrospect, General Jackson's behavior was amazing. Here was the aggressive hero of the Valley, who would later display that same aggressive energy at Second Manassas and at Chancellorsville. The opportunity to strike a decisive blow to the Union army now dangled before the Confederates, with the aggressive Jackson slated to play a key role, yet he did nothing. How could that be?

It was true that the enemy held a strong position across the swamp and that Jackson could not attack it directly, but Munford and Hampton had found alternate approaches that might allow Jackson to flank the enemy. It seems impossible that the usually aggressive Jackson did not take advantage of these.

A commander with some talent and experience, William F. "Baldy" Smith often had poor relations with superiors. He would fall in and out of favor over the course of the war and would eventually be sacked in July 1864. (loc)

Israel B. Richardson had significant pre-war experience, and he would fight at Yorktown, Seven Pines, and the Seven Days. He would be killed at the Sunken Road at Antietam in September. (loc)

White Oak Swamp marks the
nadir of Stonewall Jackson's
career, as outlined on this
Civil War Trails Marker. (cm)

A wealthy planter from South
Carolina, Wade Hampton
organized and equipped
the Hampton Legion, which
he commanded. During the
Seven Days, he led an infantry
brigade, but in July he was
assigned to J. E. B. Stuart's
cavalry. He fought well
throughout the war. Following
the war, he became governor
of his home state and was
later elected to the U.S.
Senate. (loc)

Even if he could not rout the Union troops, he could
at least tie them down, which might have made
a difference in the outcome of the battle a short
distance away at Glendale.

D. H. Hill noted that Jackson was worn down,
but Hill thought there might be other reasons for
his commander's inaction, such as Jackson wanting
to protect his troops and have others carry the load
that day. However, as historian Robert K. Krick has
noted, Jackson was not one to spare his men. Others
insinuated that Jackson could not operate effectively
under another's command of him—an opinion
Jackson would certainly disprove in the following
campaigns.

Two explanations seem the most likely. First,
Jackson was exhausted. He had fought the Valley
campaign with little rest. He then rode to Richmond
to meet with Lee and then immediately rode directly
back to the Valley. There, he took his army and led
them to Richmond, not sparing himself. One of
his artillery battalion commanders, Col. Thomas
Carter, wrote that Jackson was "physically broken
down, stupefied, and dozed with fatigue." Jackson's
aide, Sandie Pendleton, remembered that his leader
was "completely broken down."

Added to this was the fact that the Army of
Northern Virginia was basically a new army. Lee's
staff was very small, and part of the blame goes to
their poor staff work. When Jackson did not perform
as expected, a staff officer should have been sent to
find out why.

No matter the reason, Jackson's performance
this day would be the low point of his vaunted
career—and it would have serious implications for
the army's fight at Glendale.

At White Oak Swamp

If you're facing the Civil War Trails marker, and the bridge beyond, the ridge behind you that you just came down was Stonewall Jackson's position at White Oak. You'll have an easier time getting across the swamp today than Jackson's men did in 1862, although the swamp today looks pretty much like it did back then. Don't venture too near the water: aside from the turtles and beavers that are sometimes visible from the road, you might also be apt to run into a snake, and some varieties in this region *are* venomous.

A Freeman marker—its text somewhat skewed to soften Jackson's failure here—also sits nearby. Jackson was, as the tablet says, "halted by fire from Franklin's troops," but it neglects to address Jackson's subsequent failure to get across, saying only that "Jackson could not participate in the converging attacks Lee planned to deliver that day near Glendale."

➤ TO STOP 6: GLENDALE

Pull right back on to the road and continue across the bridge. You will climb another ridge, which was the Federal position at White Oak. Stay on the road until it veers to the right.

About a mile ahead, you will come to an intersection with a sign for Rt. 156 that points to the left. Turn left at the intersection. This is the Riddell's Shop/Glendale crossroads. After you have turned, you will be on Willis Church Road. Note that most of the battle occurred to your right.

You will soon see Glendale National Cemetery on your left. Pull off here.

GPS: N 37 43.738, W 77 23.406

Glendale
(Frayser's Farm)

CHAPTER ELEVEN

On the morning of June 30, the Federals were still stretched out, moving towards the James—still vulnerable—but they had been able to hold their line of defense despite some serious deficiencies: no unit cohesion, scattered corps, and no one in overall command. McClellan, once again, was not on the field, having gone to the river to meet with the navy. And again, he had left no one in charge in his stead. As at Savage's Station, his generals would have to fend for themselves.

Fortunately for the Federals, some of the most promising officers in the Army of the Potomac, brigadier generals all, were stationed near the point of greatest danger. Phil Kearny was a hard-hitting officer of great talent. Joseph Hooker—nicknamed "Fighting Joe" by the press for his aggressiveness at Williamsburg—would rise to the command of the army the next spring. Steady John Sedgwick would become the leader of the VI Corps. George Meade, currently a brigade commander, would, in one year, be placed in command of the entire army a few days before Gettysburg. With a talent pool like that at hand, fate was shining on the Federals on this last day in June.

The situation did not look as promising for the Confederates. Lee's plan at the start of the day had called for about 70,000 men to attack. Longstreet, A. P. Hill, and Huger would strike at Glendale

Concerted preservation efforts and new research have given the Glendale battlefield a new life. (cm)

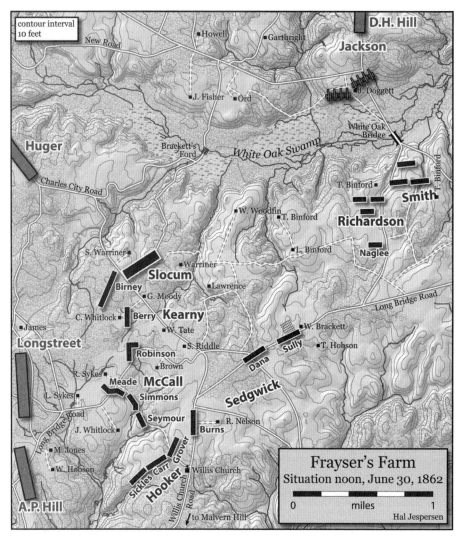

FRAYSER'S FARM—Harried for days, Federal troops took up defensive positions around Frayser's Farm. However, they were not organized by division on the field, and McClellan was not present to direct their defense. They would nonetheless put up a spirited and effective fight.

while Jackson would cross White Oak and crush the rear of the Federal line. Like a mighty vise, the Confederates had the chance to cut off and destroy a large part of McClellan's army. But of course, that plan had gone awry. Jackson had not crossed and Huger and Holmes were doing little or nothing.

The fate of the Confederates that day rested with Longstreet and A. P. Hill's 19,000 men.

As the day wore on, Lee began to grow impatient. His opportunity to inflict serious damage

The Glendale intersection was also known as "Riddell's Shop." (aw)

on the enemy seemed to be slipping away. Would McClellan be able to escape to the safety of his gunboats by the river and live to fight again? Lee's men had already suffered many casualties driving the Federals back from Richmond—would they be unable to finish the job? Lee knew the Confederacy would not likely win a long war of attrition, so he wanted to destroy McClellan now.

He rode down to see Holmes, and when he returned, Lee decided he could wait no longer: Longstreet and Hill must attack.

* * *

George McCall had positioned his three brigades on both sides of the Long Bridge Road, which, he reasoned, was a likely point of Confederate attack. To the right of the road was George Meade; to the left was Truman Seymour. Colonel Seneca G. Simmons hung back in support. A significant space existed between McCall's left and Hooker's right flank. The greatest danger lay in the gap between their divisions. If the Confederates could take advantage of this and reach the Willis Church Road, they would cause serious havoc.

The attackers faced challenging terrain. Wooded areas broke up otherwise wide, open spaces with swampy ground in some areas. Visibility was limited and communications would be difficult.

Longstreet waited for the guns that would indicate Huger's attack was underway. E. Porter Alexander lamented that "our great opportunity was practically over, and we had not yet pulled a trigger."

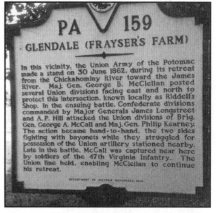

PA 159
GLENDALE (FRAYSER'S FARM)

In this vicinity, the Union Army of the Potomac made a stand on 30 June 1862, during its retreat from the Chickahominy River toward the James River. Maj. Gen. George B. McClellan posted several Union divisions facing east and north to protect this intersection, known locally as Riddell's Shop. In the ensuing battle, Confederate divisions commanded by Major Generals James Longstreet and A.P. Hill attacked the Union divisions of Brig. Gen. George A. McCall and Maj. Gen. Philip Kearney. The action became hand-to-hand, the two sides fighting with bayonets while they struggled for possession of the Union artillery stationed nearby. Late in the battle, McCall was captured near here by soldiers of the 47th Virginia Infantry. The Union line held, enabling McClellan to continue his retreat.

DEPARTMENT OF HISTORIC RESOURCES, 1994

This state historical marker is one of the few markers in the Glendale area. Only recently preserved, the battlefield is in a virgin state. The Richmond National Battlefield Park plans to create trails with more signs in the future. (dc)

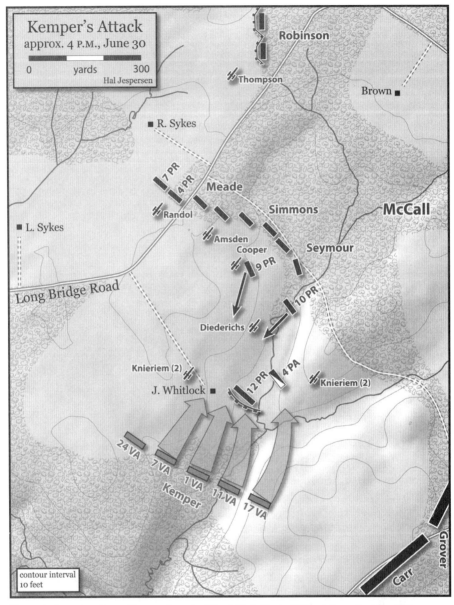

KEMPER'S ATTACK—James Kemper launched the initial attack at Glendale against the 12th Pennsylvania Reserves at the Whitlock House. While Confederates would experience initial success, lack of support and a Federal counterattack would force Kemper to pull back.

When Longstreet finally did hear something, it was not Huger, but rather the sound of the artillery duel at White Oak. Thinking it was the signal he was waiting for, he ordered the advance to begin.

Brigadier General James Kemper was the first to go in. Striking Seymour's men at the Whitlock home, Kemper's men, "rushing wildly upon the enemy," drove them back for a distance. Looking about, Kemper then realized that the Federals were all around him. He said that "the left of my line was unsupported, and greatly to my surprise and disappointment." His men charged forward, with Federal fire and canister ripping into them. One gray soldier remembered, "gap after gap yawns through the line, only to be speedily closed again." As they drew closer, they were met with "an avalanche of small arms fire." Kemper could go no further. Outnumbered, he was forced to reign in his attack and pull back.

Lawrence O'Bryan Branch's brigade, of A. P. Hill's division, was supposed to attack at the same time as Kemper, but Branch had a greater distance to march and the terrain confused him. Not having a guide, the general "took the direction whence came the shells." Like Kemper, he pushed the Federals back, but as he drove them, he, too, then found himself surrounded by troops in blue—and he, too, decided to pull back.

General George Pickett's brigade, temporarily under the command of Col. John Strange, soon arrived and advanced on Branch's right. The brigade's right had to move over "such broken ground and through an almost impassable marsh" that it slowed them. They also encountered Branch's retreating brigade. Despite this, they came within reach of their goal: to cut off the Federals by seizing the Willis Church Road.

Two of Sedgwick's brigades, Brig. Gen. Napoleon Dana's and Col. Alfred Sully's, had been sent to support the White Oak area when Jackson approached. Because the Confederates were not attacking in that sector, their troops were ordered back to relieve the pressure on McCall. Marching nearly two miles over the dust-choked road, Dana's and Sully's men arrived just in time. With Hooker also joining the fray, the Federal position in this area was secured. Kemper later lamented, "If it had been possible for these brigades to have advanced simultaneously with my own, the victory of the day would have been achieved on the right of our line with comparatively little difficulty and at an early hour."

In McCall's center, Col. Micah Jenkins attacked Lt. Frank P. Amsden's and Capt. James H. Cooper's

Micah Jenkins would add to his growing reputation at Glendale—a career that would peak on May 6, 1864, when friendly fire mortally wounded him in the Wilderness. (loc)

Truman Seymour took over command of McCall's division after the latter's capture. He led troops throughout the war, including the failed attack at Fort Wagner in 1863. Seymour was captured at the Wilderness, exchanged, and was present at Appomattox. After the war, Seymour earned a reputation as a talented artist. (loc)

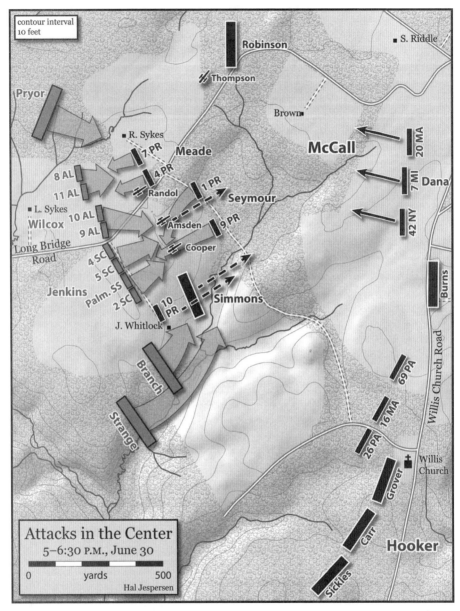

ATTACKS IN THE CENTER—Shows the action at the height of the battle. The Confederates were attempting to break through the Union guns and seize the Willis Church Road, thereby cutting off the retreating Federals. Through a series of vicious, hand–to–hand actions, the Federals were able to hold out until evening.

artillery batteries. Amsden ran out of ammunition and, unable to locate his supply wagons, had to pull out. Across the Long Bridge Road, Lt. Alanson M. Randol's guns fired in support of Cooper. As his men advanced on the Federal guns, Jenkins yelled,

"Shoot the horses!" so the cannons could not be pulled away. A northern newspaper correspondent described the scene:

> *The foe coming from the dense forests, rushed . . . with a recklessness and contempt for death that has surpassed the desperation of all other fields. In an hour like that, when men in dense masses, maddened with the excitement of battle, rush upon the fiery ordnance . . at point blank range, with charges of double-shotted grape and canister, plows a horrible furrow of flesh and gore through the living field, artillerymen, like demons incarnate, revel amid blood, groans, destruction, death, mangled forms, and fumes of hell.*

McCall rushed in troops from his left. A seesaw struggle continued, but by the end of the day, the Confederates would control the position. One of Longstreet's staff officers saw Jenkins "weeping like a child" over the slaughter of his men.

Cadmus Wilcox's Alabamians moved across the Long Bridge Road. Two of his regiments, the 9th and 10th Alabama, crossed the road in support of Jenkins. The 8th and 11th advanced on the left, toward Randol's artillery position. The 8th was met with deadly fire and halted to return it. To their left, the 11th Alabama continued on and received a punishing welcome: "a rapid discharge of grape and canister was loosed on them," one soldier said. As the Alabamians pulled back, the Federal troops counter-charged. The Confederates renewed their attack, as well, driving the retreating Federal troops directly into Randol's guns. Unable to fire at the attackers, Randol tried to pull his guns out, but the Confederates by then had shot 38 of his horses, and he lost his six pieces. As the Southerners seized the cannons, young Charlie McNeil mounted one of the guns while holding the colors—but was immediately shot. (Later, he would be found lying on the ground, pierced through his heart by a bayonet.) Randol rallied some men and was able to temporarily take the guns back.

Longstreet next sent Brig. Gen. Roger Pryor's brigade in on the left. Pryor advanced towards, James Thompson's guns, but Phil Kearny's division supported Thompson, and the Union guns held. Slocum, feeling no pressure from Huger, sent reinforcements to Kearny. Longstreet's final unit,

George Gordon Meade's men received some of the heaviest Confederate attacks at Glendale. He would be named army commander a few days before the battle of Gettysburg, where he led the Union troops to victory. (loc)

Alanson Randol was a steady soldier who fought well on many battlefields. June 30 would be a challenging day for him. (loc)

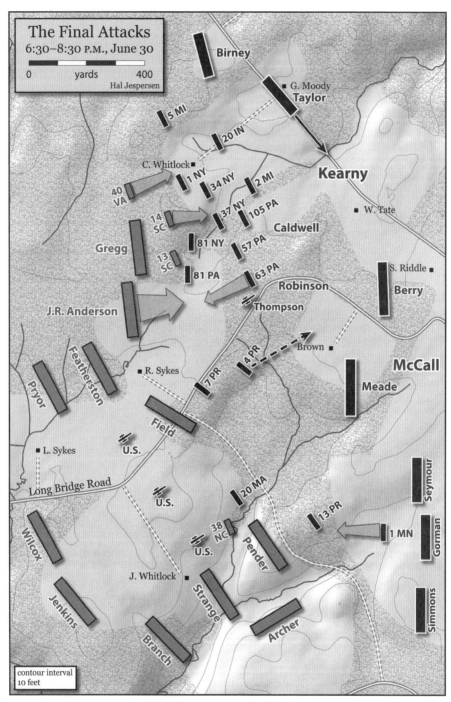

The Final Attacks
6:30–8:30 P.M., June 30

0   yards   400
Hal Jespersen

Birney

G. Moody
Taylor

5 MI

20 IN

C. Whitlock

Kearny

1 NY
34 NY
2 MI

40
VA

W. Tate

37 NY
105 PA

14
SC

Caldwell

81 NY
57 PA

Gregg

13
SC

S. Riddle

81 PA
63 PA

Berry

Robinson

J.R. Anderson

Thompson

Brown
4 PR

McCall

Featherston

R. Sykes

7 PR

Meade

Pryor

L. Sykes
U.S.

Field

Long Bridge Road

U.S.

20 MA

Seymour

Wilcox

38
NC
U.S.

13 PR

1 MN

Gorman

J. Whitlock

Pender

Strange

Jenkins

Archer

Branch

Simmons

contour interval
10 feet

THE FINAL ATTACKS—Action at the end of the day. The, final desperate Confederate attacks. The day's effort to sever the Federal retreat failed, as the Confederates lost the battle of reinforcements. Lack of involvement by Huger, Holmes, Magruder, and Jackson led to one of the great missed opportunities of the war for Lee's army.

Buttressed by reinforcements, Phil Kearny's troops held against desperate Confederate assaults. (loc)

the brigade of Winfield Featherston, then advanced, but the Federals again held.

Night was approaching, with only the remainder of A. P. Hill's men remaining to go in. The Confederates were beginning to lose the battle of numbers. Magruder's division, which might have tipped the balance in the Confederates' favor, had been ordered down to the river to support Holmes. Recalled, he would not arrive in time to support the attacks. His men had been wasted by a day of marching and counter-marching.

Hill gave the order for his 1st Brigade, under Charles W. Field, to go in "as soon as possible." Field's men attacked along both sides of the Long Bridge Road, with the 55th and 60th Virginia to the right and the 47th Virginia and the 2nd Virginia Battalion to the left. His other brigade, the 40th Virginia, had separated and was attacking even farther to the left.

Field's troops approached the batteries of Cooper and Randol, and both became scenes of seesaw fighting and slaughter. The struggle was hand to hand. Union defenders fought with bayonets, clubbed muskets, and even ramrods. Wounded men were trampled by other soldiers. The scene was terrible, consisting of desperate individual attempts to survive. A Confederate was involved in a hand-to-hand struggle with a Union officer:

Lawrence O'Bryan Branch was to meet his fate at Antietam in September. (loc)

Phil Kearny cemented his reputation as a hard fighter during the savage slugfest at Glendale. (loc)

After receiving a ball from the captain's pistol in the right arm, a sword thrust in the cheek, and a cut which laid bare the skull bone of the crown of his head, Lieut. Mickey [Michie] made a

An aggressive leader, "Fighting Joe" Hooker would rise to an ill-fated command of the army in 1863. (loc)

desperate thrust with his bright and flashing sword which penetrated and passed through the body of the gallant captain, who staggered back and in a moment fell a lifeless corpse.

Randol's battery, with its guns "whose grim mouths were black from hurling death," finally succumbed. Although the fight at Cooper's artillery position continued, night soon fell, and the Federals began to pull back toward Malvern Hill. The Confederates took the field, but the Federals had held out long enough for their army to escape.

For so little gain, both side paid a terrific price: of an estimated 42,700 men involved, losses ranged between 6,300 to 7,400 killed, wounded, or missing for both sides.

The night was one that would be long remembered. Joseph Hooker wrote:

From the torches we could see that the enemy was busy all night long in searching for his wounded, but up to daylight the following morning there had been no apparent diminution in the heart-rending cries and groans of the wounded. The unbroken, mournful wail of human suffering was all that we heard from Glendale during that long, dismal night.

Not only the wounded suffered. "Half-starved men, the few clothes we wear, were soaked with persperation, grime and powdersmoke," one soldier of the 7th New York remembered, "and yet so cold that our teeth were chattering, burning thirsts and dry throats and toungs. A kingdom for a piece of bread and a drink of water!"

June 30, 1862, represented one of the greatest lost opportunities of the war for the Confederates. Not only did Huger, Holmes, and Jackson fail to contribute, Magruder's troops were wasted. Longstreet's attacks were piecemeal, and Hill's men were perhaps held back too long. Despite all of that, they came close to realizing their goal. Still, the Federal army, after a tenacious and desperate effort, held on to fight another day. Phil Kearny saw the situation clearly when he said the battle at Glendale was "one of the most desperate of the war, the one most fatal if lost."

It had been a long, anxious week. The largest

battle had been at Gaines's Mill, but the most critical had been the one fought at Glendale. The price of the missed opportunity would cost the Confederates greatly—beginning the very next day on the gentle slope of Malvern Hill.

At Glendale

The foundation is all that remains of the Frayser/Nelson home. (cm)

Willis Church presents a well-kept entry today. (dc)

Many Civil War battles have multiple names, but Glendale might have the most. While generally recognized as Glendale, in the South it was best known as "Frayser's farm" (sometimes spelled as Frazier's) after the family that had once operated a farm here. It was also termed "Nelson's farm," after the then-current owners. Other names include Riddell's Shop, White Oak, Charles City Crossroads, Charles City Road, Long Bridge Road, New Market Road, and Willis Church Road. In 2006, with several housing projects under development in the area, Glendale appeared on the Civil War Trust's list of most endangered battlefields. In more than a century and a quarter, only a single acre of core battlefield had been preserved, although the Trust had managed to save several properties on the battlefield's fringe.

"Late in 2005, the first piece of Glendale's remarkable reclamation puzzle fell into place, when the Civil War Trust acquired a crucial 43 acre tract at the very heart of the battlefield," said the Trust's website.

Soon thereafter, the Trust found itself able to negotiate for more land—nearly 600 acres, all told.

National Park Service Historian Robert E. L. Krick said, in a Trust release, that the preservation success at Glendale "defies comparison.

"There has been nothing like it before in Virginia . . ." Krick said. "Never before in modern times has anyone preserved a major battlefield virtually from scratch. . . ." Once upon a time, he said, "one could not even find a safe roadside pull-off at which to pause for basic orientation; now, incredibly and suddenly, almost all of the battlefield will be accessible."

At the time of this writing, Richmond National Battlefield is still working on its site plan for the property, but occasionally, park staff members offer tours. Plans are in the works to construct a walking tour along with signage in the near future, so stay tuned. You will definitely want to take advantage of the walking trail once it becomes available.

Otherwise, there's little to see. The modest remains of the Nelson farm sit in the middle of a field adjacent to the visitor center: a simple square foundation flanked by several trees.

In the summer, the cemetery building serves as a visitor center. Check in advance for operating hours. The building houses a museum that, although small, is well worth the stop. A knowledgeable ranger is posted here, plus the museum contains an electronic map that demonstrates troop movements for both the Glendale and Malvern Hill battles. When the museum is open, there are restrooms available.

The cemetery is of interest, and note that there is a Medal of Honor veteran from the Vietnam War buried here: Michael Fleming Folland (1949-1969) of the 3rd Infantry Regiment of the 199th Infantry Brigade. On July 3, 1969, during fighting in the Long Khanh province of Vietnam, Folland threw himself on an enemy grenade, smothering its blast and saving the lives of his fellow soldiers.

Top: Glendale National Cemetery sits adjacent to the battlefield visitor center. Approximately half of the 2,000 men buried in the cemetery remain unidentified. The cemetery closed to new interments in 1970. (al)

Bottom: The Richmond National Battlefield Park's visitor center, once the cemetery superintendent's lodge, is open during summer months. (aw)

According to his Medal of Honor citation:

"Cpl. Folland distinguished himself while serving as an ammunition bearer with the weapons platoon of Company D, during a reconnaissance patrol mission. As the patrol was moving through a dense jungle area, it was caught in an intense crossfire from heavily fortified and concealed enemy ambush positions. As the patrol reacted to neutralize the ambush, it became evident that the heavy weapons could not be used in the cramped fighting area. Cpl. Folland dropped his recoilless rifle ammunition, and ran forward to join his commander in an assault on the enemy bunkers. The assaulting force moved forward until it was pinned down directly in front of the heavily fortified bunkers by machine gun fire. Cpl. Folland stood up to draw enemy fire on himself and to place suppressive fire on the enemy positions while his commander attempted to destroy the machine gun positions with grenades. Before the officer could throw a grenade, an enemy grenade landed in the position. Cpl. Folland alerted his comrades and his commander hurled the grenade from the position. When a second enemy grenade landed in the position, Cpl. Folland again shouted a warning to his fellow soldiers. Seeing that no one could reach the grenade and realizing that it was about to explode, Cpl. Folland, with complete disregard for his safety, threw himself on the grenade. By his dauntless courage, Cpl. Folland saved the lives of his comrades although he was mortally wounded by the explosion. . . ."

Just down the road from the visitor center, you will pass Willis Church. The original structure burned after the war but has since been recreated.

▶ TO STOP 7: THE PARSONAGE

As you leave the cemetery, continue in the direction you were going on Willis Church Road. Almost immediately, you will pass the site of the historic Willis Church (on your right). In 1.4 miles, you will come to the Park Service's "Parsonage" parking lot. Turn left into the lot and park.

GPS: N 37 41.319, W 77 24.994

Michael Folland's Medal of Honor citation reads, in part: **"For conspicuous gallantry and intrepidity in action at the risk of his life above and beyond the call of duty."** (dc)

Grave at Willis Church (dc)

The Federal Retreat

CHAPTER TWELVE

JULY 1, 1862

Following the battle on the 30th, McClellan sent a telegram to Washington telling of "another day of desperate fighting." Claiming that he faced greatly superior numbers, he said his army had "done all that men can do." In his usual defeatist tone, he went on: "If none of us escape we shall at least have done honor to the country. I shall do my best to save the Army."

Two days earlier, in a telegram to Secretary of War Edwin Stanton, he had written, "If I save this Army now I can tell you plainly that I owe no thanks to you or any other persons in Washington—you have done your best to sacrifice this Army."

Early on the morning of July 1, McClellan rode along the line that Fitz John Porter had established on Malvern Hill, enjoying as he always did the cheers of the men. Then he left for Haxall's Landing, where he would spend the remainder of the day scouting the position for his new base. As had been his wont during the week, he left no one in overall command. This day, however, it would not be a problem, as Porter was in *de facto* command after having set up the defense.

The position the Federal army occupied on the morning of July 1 was probably its strongest of the war. In fact, it was nearly impregnable. A visitor to the site today might be disappointed, expecting a steep hill much like Marye's Heights at Fredericksburg, but the slight, gentle rise was an artilleryman's dream. The field had a slight slope, which gave the gunners an excellent field of fire and freedom from worry that the enemy could hide below the elevation of the guns. The view was open,

The Willis parsonage, a prominent landmark on the battlefield, burned down in 1988, leaving behind only twin chimneys, which still stand.
(cm)

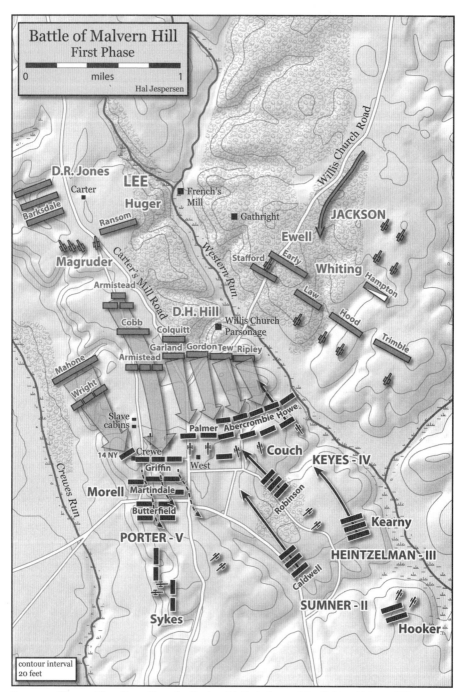

BATTLE OF MALVERN HILL (FIRST PHASE)—During the first phase of the fight at Malvern Hill, John Magruder attacked—triggered by a miscommunication—and D. H. Hill followed. Confederate troops would pay a steep price.

At this stage of the war, the Confederates still fielded a number of 6-pounder cannon, which had become obsolete because they were no match for the power and range of the 12-pounder smoothbore Napoleons and rifled pieces used by the Federals. During the coming winter, Lee would have these melted down and recast into larger guns. (dc)

with corn only waist-high and recently harvested wheat standing in neat shocks.

About 900 yards wide, the farmland had space for about 35 to 40 guns at the crest of the slope. Ten and 20-pounder Parrott-rifled cannon and 12-pounder Napoleon guns dominated the scene. Heavier 30-pounder Parrott rifles and 4.5-inch Rodmans waited in support, and the Federal gunboats on the James floated within range.

Two infantry divisions, those of George W. Morell and Darius N. Couch, had about 17,500 men posted to defend the guns. On the left flank, the land dropped precipitously and was aptly named Malvern Cliffs. There, George Sykes posted his division atop the top.

The Federal right was stationed on what was probably the most vulnerable terrain, but divisions from the corps of Samuel P. Heintzelman, Edwin V. Sumner, and William B. Franklin guarded it. McCall's division stood by in reserve. Nearly the entire Federal army supported the position. Viewing the front of the Federal defense, Confederate Maj. Gen. D. H. Hill said, "If Gen. McClellan is there in strength, we had better leave him alone." Unfortunately for the Confederate army, Lee would not heed Hill's cautionary words.

Lee's frustration, building over the course of days, nearly steamed out of him. McClellan was

Federal gunboats shelled Malvern Hill, adding to the overwhelming Union firepower. (loc)

escaping. This might be his last chance to damage the Union army—but how to get at them?

As Jackson arrived on the field at Glendale, Lee ordered him to follow the Union army down the Willis Church Road and establish his position on what would become the Confederate left, at the Poindexter Farm. D. H. Hill would set up immediately to Jackson's right, in the area of the Willis Church Parsonage. Magruder and Huger were to follow and take up position on Hill's right, respectively. Longstreet and A. P. Hill's men, exhausted after the fighting of the previous day, would make up the army's reserve.

As had become so typical during the week, the Southern troops did not get in the proper positions at the appointed times. Magruder had been ordered down the Quaker Road in pursuit of the retreating Federals. Unfortunately for him, he became another victim of poor maps and a confused guide. He was attempting to follow the Quaker Road to the front, but there was more than one road called "Quaker" in the vicinity, and Magruder's guide led him down the wrong one, moving away from the battlefield. Longstreet noticed this and pointed it out to Magruder but did not think he had the authority to order "Prince John" to change his course. Soon, having been convinced of the error, Magruder doubled back and marched down the Willis Church ("Quaker") Road, eventually arriving late on the field.

As Longstreet surveyed the scene, he clearly saw the dominating Federal artillery. He also noticed something else: an elevated point on the right from which the Confederates could set up

Confederates marched up a long, open, gentle incline into the face of a dominating Federal artillery position. (kw)

artillery. If Jackson could do the same on the left, it was possible that they could converge their fire on Porter's guns, disrupting them and possibly setting the stage for a successful infantry attack. Longstreet recommended this to Lee, who told his commanders to move the guns into position.

Brigadier General Lewis Armistead's brigade was on a knoll at the front and was in the best position to observe the effect of the Southern artillery fire. Early in the afternoon, Lee's assistant adjutant, R. H. Chilton, delivered an order to Lee's commanders stating that if the guns had the desired effect and broke the Federal lines, Armistead's men were to "Charge with a yell. Do the same." This would be the rather strange signal for a general assault all along the line.

Unfortunately for Lee's army, the plan would quickly unravel.

Part of the difficulty stemmed from the way the Confederate artillery was distributed. The army did not have a large reserve of cannon; rather, the guns were allocated at the brigade level. That meant that in order to get them into position, they would have to be brought up in small quantities, often from behind the brigades they were assigned to. This, of course, would take time, moving them up through their brigades and getting them into position. What artillery reserve the army did have—14 batteries— was under the command of the none-too-competent Brig. Gen. William Pendleton. A former West Point cadet who had graduated fifth in the class of 1830, Pendleton had become an Episcopalian minister, but left his church at the beginning of the war and

The Confederates attacked from the woods in the distance across this open field. The woodline to the left was farther back during the war. (aw)

offered his services to the young Confederacy. Pendleton was unable to get many of his guns to the front this day because, he said, he could not locate Lee to receive orders.

Because the Confederate guns came to into position piecemeal, it was a simple matter for the Federal artillery on the crest of the hill to concentrate on batteries as they were being set up. With few guns making it to the front, and the Southerners unable to mass any fire on the right side of the line, the Confederate artillery in that sector had no chance.

On the left, Jackson's chief of artillery, Col. Stapleton Crutchfield, was ill, so Jackson—a former artillery instructor—took to placing the guns himself. He had no better luck than his compatriots on the other end of the line. The guns were too few and too slow in coming up. General William Whiting of Jackson's division placed his guns in position under protest, stating, "These few guns will not be able to live in the field five minutes."

"Obey your orders . . . willingly and promptly," Jackson replied.

The Confederate fire was so ineffective that D. H. Hill said the effort "was of the most farcical character."

Federal guns were dominating, reaching the Confederates as they rose out of the woods. The range of their cannons and the size of their payloads also often exceeded that of Lee's artillery because some of the Southern guns were obsolete 6-pounders and howitzers. Confederate batteries were destroyed; men and horses were killed and wounded. Artillerist R. W. Royall wrote that it was "almost miraculous how any of us escaped." The only relief Confederates experienced came when Porter ordered the Union gunboats to stop firing because some of the shells were dropping short and killing his men. Overall, though, it was one of the best days of the war for Federal artillery.

By 3:00 in the afternoon, it was becoming apparent that the Confederate cannonade was not having the desired effect. In his report of the battle, Longstreet wrote that he "understood that we would not be able to attack the enemy that day, inasmuch as his position was too strong to admit of it." Lee sent for him, and together they rode around to the left, looking for a way to turn McClellan's flank. Lee ordered Longstreet to shift troops to that location.

However, according to Longstreet, the Confederate commander did not send out a communication cancelling his original attack orders.

Intense close-range fighting occurred near these slave cabins, which no longer exist. This image was taken in the 1880s to accompany a series of articles that appeared in *Century Magazine.* (rnbp)

Around 4 p.m., Lee received an unexpected message. Union wagons and men could be seen in motion on the hill—could they be retreating? Magruder had arrived late to the field and was made aware of the order to attack if Armistead's men advanced "with a yell." Prince John had disappointed Lee two days back at Savage's Station, and at Glendale he was not a factor. Today, he was late to the field and had taken morphine for acute indigestion, but he determined not to let his commander down again on this day.

Several of Armistead's regiments began pushing back Federal sharpshooters, but Magruder saw this and interpreted it as an advance. He sent his aide, Capt. A. G. Dickinson, to tell Lee that Armistead seemed to be attacking and succeeding. Around the same time, on the other end of the Confederate line, Chase Whiting saw some Federals pulling back. These were merely Sumner's troops pulling back to avoid the limited Confederate artillery fire, but to Whiting, it must have seemed that the Federals were beginning to retreat, so he, too sent word to the commanding general.

Private Edwin Jemison was killed at Malvern Hill. His photo has become one of the most iconic images from the war. (loc)

Could this be Lee's opportunity? If so, it could be his last chance. He decided he must act *now*.

He sent a message to Magruder via Captain Dickinson: "Gen. Lee expects you to advance rapidly. He says it is reported the enemy is getting off. Press forward your whole line and follow up Armistead's successes."

Simple misunderstandings would lead to a catastrophe this day.

At the Parsonage

The West house sits atop the crest of the same ridge where Federals positioned their devastating artillery. (cm)

During the battle, D. H. Hill's men occupied the land you are standing on. The house visible in the distance is the West house. If you face back in the direction of Glendale, Jackson's men were nearby to the right rear, on the Poindexter farm, which is private property.

Across the street from the parking lot, you will see two chimneys—all that remains of the historic Willis parsonage, which belonged to the Willis Methodist Church (back on the Glendale battlefield). Before the battle, a compassionate Federal soldier went to the house to remove the inhabitants. During the battle, Colonel W. Gaston Meares of North Carolina, who was in the parsonage's yard, died when an incoming shell hit him.

The parsonage was one of the first properties purchased by a preservation organization—the former Association for the Preservation of Civil War Sites, a predecessor of the Civil War Trust. "It initiated the momentum that has produced repeated preservation successes here at Malvern Hill in more recent years," explained Park Service Historian Robert E. L. Krick in a Civil War Trust video, "which in turn has produced a battlefield that is protected almost in its entirety and has more integrity than any other battlefield in this part of Virginia."

The parking lot also serves as the trailhead for a one-and-a-half-mile hiking trail that winds across the battlefield. If you follow the trail across the road toward the chimneys and into the woods, it will bring you to one of the Confederate artillery positions. The path then circles up toward the

Federal position, allowing visitors to walk in Confederates' footsteps as they made their doomed assault.

➤ TO STOP 8: MALVERN HILL

Turn left out of the parking lot. Follow the road up the ridge until you see the turn-off for another parking area. This is the Union position on the Malvern Hill battlefield.

GPS: N 37 41.319, W 77 24.994

The Malvern Hill hiking trail has two trailheads: one at the parsonage and one at the Federal position on the crest of the hill. More than a dozen interpretive markers along the way help explain the action. (cm)

Confederate artillery on display belies the difficulty artillerists faced in keeping their pieces on the field and active. Federal dominance kept sweeping them from the field. (kw)

Hurricane on the Hill

CHAPTER THIRTEEN

JULY 1, 1862

John Magruder had his orders to advance, and advance he would. Unfortunately, his troops were not in position to attack yet, and he only had Huger's brigades of Ambrose Wright and Lewis Armistead directly on hand. Coming up were two more of Huger's brigades, William Mahone's and Robert Ransom's, although Huger himself was not present. He was in the rear, back at the Long Bridge Road, taking offense because his troops had been ordered about that day without consultation.

Magruder ordered the advance. One Confederate remembered looking at the strength of the Federal position he would walk towards: "I could scarcely believe my own eyes as I looked upon it." Wright's men moved forward, supported by Armistead's. As they attacked, Armistead and Mahone's troops quickly became pinned down, and these men felt the focused fury of the enemy's guns.

In Magruder's sector the field rose gently toward the Union position on the crest, with only a large swale to protect attackers. As the Confederates advanced, the only protection they would find was in that depression. The Federals took full advantage of this by posting their guns to the front where they could sweep the field. Infantry support—in this case, one of George Morell's brigades led by Charles Griffin—waited behind the guns. If needed, they could move forward, in front of the artillery to inflict devastating rifle fire on any attackers unwise enough to come within range.

As the Confederates began their assault, Union artillerists stacked ammunition by their guns and began firing as quickly as possible, often without stopping to "sponge" the bores of their cannons—a very risky proposition, as the ammunition could

This battery—part of Adelbart Ames's guns on the Federal left—remained in place during the entire battle. (cw)

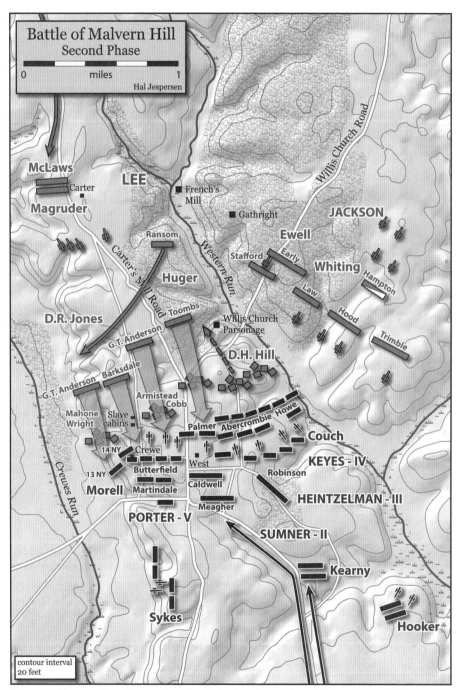

BATTLE OF MALVERN HILL (SECOND PHASE)—Following the repulse of Magruder and D. H. Hill, Lee launched wave after wave of additional attacks. Federals rebuffed each in turn.

explode prematurely. Cannoneers were ordered to fire at the feet of the enemy to ensure that their shots did not sail over the attackers' heads. A Federal soldier wrote that the Union guns filled the air "with smoke of bursting shells whose fragments plowed the ground in front," cutting huge gaps in the Confederate lines. Douglas Southall Freeman would comment that the Southerners were "[f]ull of the ardor of 1862 that made all the Confederates regard an infantry charge on a battery as the supreme glory of war."

Federal troops rush to meet the Confederate onslaught. (loc)

Magruder continually ordered regiments and brigades to attack as they became available, rather than gathering them for a massed attack. The carnage was horrendous. Never having adequate strength to launch an effective, concerted assault, Magruder fed his men repeatedly into the meat grinder. When Robert Ransom's large brigade reached the field, it was ordered forward and suffered 499 casualties out of a total of nearly 3,000 men.

A Federal artillerist was sickened by the effect of the guns. He said the shells "cut roads through them some places ten feet wide."

The Confederate artillery, generally ineffective, did manage to cause some damage. Someone saw a Federal captain hit by a shell, which exploded inside him, throwing his arm 60 feet in the air: "[H]is flesh was scattered around, smoke from the explosion rising from his body." Of the continuous firing of the guns, a soldier remembered, "The earth trembled and shook as though an earthquake had occurred." Another veteran added, "The eternal fires below seemed to us to have been turned loosed about us." Union batteries would be replaced by others as they ran out of ammunition. Lieutenant Adelbert Ames, who commanded Battery A of the 5th U.S. Light Artillery, termed his fire "very effective" and said the Confederates who attacked "were entirely cut up." He was determined to fight the thing out. Rather than pull back his guns, as was typical when a battery ran out of ammunition, he continuously sent his caissons to the rear for more. His battery fired an estimated 1,392 rounds that day.

A battery commander at Bull Run, Hunt rose to become the preeminent artillery commander of the Civil War. He is most famous for his use of artillery during the battles of Malvern Hill and Gettysburg. (loc)

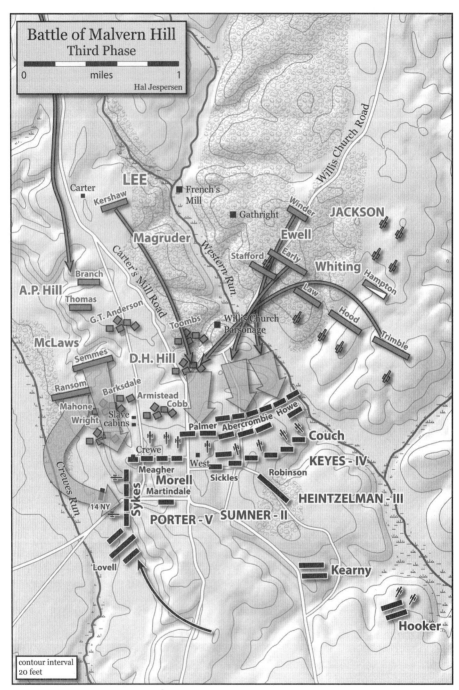

BATTLE OF MALVERN HILL (THIRD PHASE)—During the final assaults by the Confederates on the Federal left, Jackson's men joined the attack on the right. A deep ravine on the Federal left, in particular, turned into a shooting gallery. By the end of the battle, Federals held the field.

* * *

On the east side of the road, things unfolded somewhat differently, owing mainly to the terrain. While there was only the one depression to protect the attackers on the west side, to the east, there were a number of depressions the Confederates could reach to avoid Federal fire. Union Gen. Darius Couch, whose men had not seen any action thus far over the seven days of battle, realized this and moved his brigades—Albion Howe, John Abercrombie, and Innis Palmer—in front of the guns in his sector in order to keep the attackers from reaching the shelter offered by the terrain.

D. H. Hill, seeing Magruder's attack, ordered his men forward in support. He had some 8,200 men in five brigades, but like Magruder, Hill was unable to send them in one massed attack. He also did not coordinate with Magruder.

As the Confederates advanced, the Yankee infantry fired off their allocated 60 rounds per man. Ripley and Col. Alfred H. Colquitt drove forward but were pushed back, losing more than 600 men between them. Colonel John Gordon led General Rodes's brigade in place of its wounded commander. The 3rd Alabama lost 56 percent of its men in the attack. George Anderson had no better fortune with his brigade.

As the assaults continued and Couch's men began to run out of ammunition, he called to Porter for support. Daniel Sickles's New York "Excelsior" Brigade came up in relief, followed later by the 61st New York, led by Francis Barlow. The 5th New Hampshire also came up in support. The Federal line held.

D. H. Hill would lose 1,756 of his men this day in fruitless assaults

The Confederate attacks continued as the day neared its end. Two brigades from Lafayette McLaws's division advanced, accompanied by remnants from other units. "A terrific storm of grapeshot greeted [the enemy] as they came on," a Yankee soldier remembered. "Again and again the cannon blazed forth their murderous rage . . . ranks fell down, actually shattered and blown to pieces; yet still the brave fellows came on, closer and closer."

On the Federal left, as the Confederates

Artillerist Adelbart Ames would later switch to infantry in order to earn promotions. He fought through the war, and led the successful attack against Fort Fisher in 1865. He became the governor of Mississippi, as well as a U.S. senator. During the Spanish-American War, Ames left retirement and was again a general. He died in 1933. (rnbp)

Within seven months of the Seven Days, Darius Couch would be second in command of the Army of the Potomac. However, following Chancellorsville, Couch requested reassignment after arguing with his superior, Joseph Hooker. (loc)

The Federal left rested in front of a deep ravine that offered ample protection from Confederate advance. (cm)

approached the slave cabins near the Crew house, the Irish Brigade under Brig. Gen. Thomas F. Meagher moved in front of the guns to meet them. Bitter fighting ensued, but in the end, the attackers pulled back. The Union line would not be broken this day.

Lee, who was in the center of the Confederate line, watched events unfold and then spin out of his control. He had not wanted a battle on these terms, yet there it was. The Confederates gained nothing tactically and lost horrendous numbers: More than 5,600 Confederates were lost, including 869 killed. Surprisingly, the Federals also suffered severe casualties. They lost some 3,000 men, with 314 killed.

Perplexed, Lee rode to Magruder and asked, "Gen. Magruder, why did you attack?"

"In obedience to your orders," the unfortunate Magruder replied, "twice repeated."

Errors in communication were extremely costly this day.

D. H. Hill would say that the Confederates "[d]id not move together and were beaten in detail. . . . [I]t was not war—it was murder."

In the end, the Federals won a tactical success, but Lee had gained the strategic—but extremely costly—victory.

At Malvern Hill

The terrain at Malvern Hill is very close to what it would have looked like in 1862; in fact it's one of America's best-preserved battlefields. As you stand in the parking lot facing the field, look to your left. To match 1862, the woodline should be further back, but the Park Service cannot remove these trees due to environmental regulations. Other than that the terrain is accurate.

Directly to your front you will see a group of 6 guns. This is the approximate position of Adelbert Ames's battery during the battle.

The house to your left is the Crew house, which was reconstructed after a postwar fire. Though it is private property, you may access markers to the right of the house. It is highly recommended that you take the walking tour to get a feel for the battle. If the crops are growing, the path to the Confederate side (Magruder's) is to your left, at the woodline.

To your right is the West house. This is not the historic building, although the house was constructed on part of the original foundation. Notice the difference between battlefields in the summer of 1864 (such as Cold Harbor) and those of 1862. The Federals had been on Malvern Hill since the previous day, but made no effort to entrench. Two years later they would have likely constructed strong earthworks. Cross the road and read the signs; this was Couch's position during the battle. Part of the walking tour also goes from this area to D. H. Hill's sector at the parsonage. The path is near the woodline. Watch your step, as the ground can be uneven in places.

Dan Sickles's New York "Excelsior" Brigade moved to the front to support Darius Couch's men. Several of the men from the brigade posed for this photo just days before the battle at Malvern Hill. (loc)

On the 150th anniversary of the battle, the Richmond National Battlefield Park's chief historian made an interesting comment about how the battle differed on either side of the main road. On the west side of the road, there was little cover other than the swale visible if you walk the trail. The Confederates on this side were almost totally exposed and were swept by the Federal artillery. To the east side, there are a number of nooks for troops to hide. The Union troops moved well forward there; signs, which you'll see as you walk the battlefield, describe this.

It is critically important to visit battlefields, and the preservation of Malvern Hill makes a prime case in point. Without walking the ground, it is difficult to truly understand the battle or get a sense of what the troops felt. You are encouraged to walk this field slowly and in its entirety. Imagine what happened here. You will find yourself transported back to July 1, 1862.

If you would like to see the video of the anniversary talk, it's available on You Tube at https://www.youtube.com/watch?v=38j1xUeCSPI.

Dawn of the Army of Northern Virginia

CHAPTER FOURTEEN

JULY 2, 1862

When the Confederates arose on July 2, they discovered that the enemy had vanished. In their place were the thousands of dead and wounded, with their all-too-familiar screams, cries, and moans. The scene was appalling. One veteran wrote that the wounded on the field created a "singular crawling effect."

As distressing as the scene was, Lee could not be distracted. He had to quickly determine what McClellan might do next. There was no time to waste.

For their part, some of the Federal commanders opposed pulling the army back to McClellan's new base at the river. They had defeated the Confederates soundly on the previous day. Might this not be a good opportunity to go over to the offensive and strike the enemy while they were disorganized? Fitz John Porter wrote that they had inflicted "on the enemy a blow which under other circumstances might have been followed up to a decisive victory."

However, McClellan wanted to get his army to Harrison's Landing, where the navy's gunboats could protect them, and where he could rest, refit, and possibly reinforce his still powerful army. Phil Kearny, by nature aggressive, wanted to attack, and reportedly said the order to retreat "can only be prompted by cowardice or treason." Nonetheless, McClellan's army, exhausted after a week of fighting, marched towards the new base on the James River. The enormous mass of men, horses,

Berkeley Plantation, the ancestral home of the Harrison family—including a signer of the Declaration of Independence and two U.S. presidents—swarmed with Federal soldiers once McClellan shifted his supply base to Harrison's Landing along the James River. (cm)

wagons, artillery, and cattle clogged the roads as they continued their flight.

Anxious to find out where McClellan was going, Lee sent Stuart east to determine if the Federals were moving back down the Peninsula. Another possibility was that they would cross the James and move against the rail center at Petersburg. Such a move could cut the Confederate supply line from the south. Lee sent Holmes to Drewry's Bluff to keep an eye out in case that was McClellan's plan. Longstreet and Jackson, meanwhile, were to follow McClellan.

Regardless of the Confederate efforts, the Federals made good their escape, and by July 4, they sat safely at their new base at Harrison's Landing.

* * *

In a July 7 letter, McClellan provided unwanted political advice to President Lincoln, counseling that "neither confiscation of property, political executions of persons, territorial organization of states or forcible abolition of slavery should be contemplated for a moment." To get a better measure of the situation, Lincoln visited McClellan at Harrison's Landing the next day, July 8. McClellan thought that his army should make a new effort against Richmond, but in a letter to Edwin Stanton, he said, "reinforcements should be sent to me rather much over than much less than 100,000 men."

An exasperated Lincoln decided to make some changes. From the other Federal forces in Virginia, Lincoln created a new army under Maj. Gen. John Pope. He also brought Maj. Gen. Henry W. Halleck in from the West and assigned him to overall command of all of the Union armies. Lincoln immediately sent Halleck to Harrison's Landing to see if he could get the ball rolling again.

McClellan proposed taking his army across the James and cutting off the railroads approaching Richmond from the south (a strategy that General in Chief Ulysses S. Grant would adopt two years later), but Halleck thought this too risky. Typically, McClellan also began to have doubts, thinking that the Confederates could bring forces in from the West to join their already-massive army. He quickly dropped his plan.

With McClellan hunkered down along the James River, Lincoln looked for alternatives to carry the war in the east forward. His choice of Maj. Gen. Henry Halleck (left) to serve as general in chief seemed, at first, inspired. "Old Brains," as Halleck was known, had a reputation as a great military mind, bolstered by several battlefield wins in the Western Theater. Lincoln also brought Maj. Gen. John Pope (right) to the east. Pope, who had strung together a series of victories along the Mississippi, would head a newly formed Army of Virginia. McClellan would see both appointments as personal affronts. (loc)(loc)

McClellan once again called for reinforcements, but Halleck, having little faith in McClellan, decided instead to pull the Army of the Potomac out of Harrison's Landing and join it with Pope's command. He issued orders to that effect on August 3.

On August 5, McClellan made one last abortive attempt to move towards Richmond. He sent Joseph Hooker and 17,000 men to Malvern Hill, but when the Confederates responded in force, Hooker's troops were recalled.

Lee received word that General Pope's army was moving south. So confident was Lee that he had the cautious McClellan boxed in that on August 13 he sent Jackson, leading the commands of Ewell and Winder, to "suppress" the "miscreant" Pope. Jackson's group would be augmented by the division of A. P. Hill. Although Jackson's performance the previous week had been disappointing, Lee was well aware of the abilities that general had demonstrated in the Valley campaign and maintained confidence in him.

On August 13, Lee ordered Longstreet to take ten brigades and head north in support, and in late August, the Confederates crushed Pope at the old battlefield of Manassas. In September, they would cross the Potomac into Maryland.

* * *

Meanwhile, the week of the Seven Days' had been an amazing reversal for the Confederates. On June 25, their backs were to the wall, with McClellan's massive siege guns nearly within range of Richmond. Doom shadowed the Southern

Lee had struggled to land a crushing blow against McClellan, suffering severely in the process, as the litter of bodies across the Malvern Hill landscape illustrated. This sign, telling part of that story, sits along the Malvern Hill hiking trail. (dc)

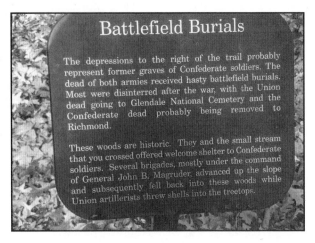

doorstep. By July 2, Lee and his army had driven the Federals to an encampment some 25 miles distant from the city.

However, the cost had been appalling. The Confederates suffered nearly 3,500 deaths. Sixteen thousand men were wounded and about 900 missing. A total of about 20,000 men had been lost. Though some of these men would return to the army, many others never would. The Confederacy could not afford such casualties, but the times were desperate. Lee saw no alternative. He had to drive McClellan from Richmond and save the capital—and, indeed, Lee had done just that.

In its repulse, the Northern army also suffered greatly. Some 1,700 were killed, 8,000 wounded, and 6,000 missing, for an approximate total of 15,700.

The Seven Days' seemed a brilliant Confederate victory, yet Robert E. Lee, son of "Light-Horse Harry," hero of the Revolutionary War, was far from satisfied. He knew that the South had missed a chance at a greater success, perhaps one that might have ended the war. "Under ordinary circumstances," he said in his official report, "the Federal Army should have been destroyed." That, of course, is pure speculation, but others, too, saw the lost opportunity. In 1882 Cadmus Wilcox wrote a letter that was published in the *Philadelphia Times Weekly*: "[H]ad the orders of the Confederate Commander been carried out as contemplated . . ." he wrote, "[it] would have been most disastrous, in all probability, to the Federals."

In the years after the war, a sketch artist captured the pastoral landscape that had returned to Malvern Hill. This perspective was captured near the Federal left. (rnbp)

In his *Military Memoirs of a Confederate,* Porter Alexander lamented the failure at Glendale, but his sentiments applied to the entire campaign:

> *I have often thought that in his retrospect of the war no one day of the whole four years would seem to him more unfortunate. . . . It was, undoubtedly, the opportunity of his life, for the Confederacy was then in its prime, with more men available than ever before or after. And at no other period would the moral or the physical effect of a victory have been so great as upon this occasion.*

Postwar scholars agreed with the assessment, as typified by Lee's early biographer, Douglas Southall Freeman, who called Glendale

> *the bitterest disappointment that Lee had ever sustained, and one that he could not conceal. Many times thereafter he was to discover a weak point in his adversary's line or a mistake in his antagonist's plan, but never again was he to find the enemy in full retreat across his front. Victories in the field were to be registered, but two years of open campaign were not to produce another situation where envelopment seemed possible. He had only that one day for a Cannae, and his army was not ready for it.*

Lee's army was new to him. He had little time to develop the organization he ended up needing on the battlefield. Once the fighting opened, time was of the essence, and he had to act. After the campaign, he immediately began taking measures to strengthen his command structure. Benjamin Huger, who had accomplished nothing, was sent away, as was Theophilus Holmes. The unfortunate John Magruder, who seemed the victim of bad luck from June 29 on, was sent west.

It might be argued that Lee treated Magruder unfairly or that he was a victim of circumstances. A keen judge of men, though, Lee saw something more. Whether exhausted, ill, or both, Magruder did not control his emotions in the manner the usually reserved Lee felt necessary for a leader, and Lee would not have that in one of his top commanders.

Jackson, who had contributed little during the week, was spared. Lee had viewed his performance in the Valley campaign and made one of his wisest decisions by retaining him. Lee saw a fighter in Longstreet, who would grow to be one his most relied-upon subordinates, Lee's "Old War Horse." Longstreet performed well at Gaines's Mill and was the most reliable commander at Glendale. He seemed to handle a large body of troops better than anyone during the campaign. Lee would also keep his eye on A. P. Hill, who though a fighter was new to division command and perhaps a bit impetuous.

Lee recognized, as well, that his span of control was simply too wide: too many officers reported to him directly. With no corps structure authorized by the Confederate Congress, he divided his army into two wings: Jackson led the divisions that went out to seek Pope while Longstreet commanded those that temporarily remained in the Richmond area. Lee was comfortable with two commands under him, and only changed the structure after Jackson's death at Chancellorsville, when he was unsure of the capabilities of someone to replace him.

The week of the Seven Days' also drew attention to another critical shortcoming: Lee's staff was simply too small and used ineffectively. His plans were brilliant, but their execution was poor. A strong staff might have been able to ensure that field officers carried out Lee's orders in a more timely and effective manner.

The Seven Days' campaign was a turning point in several ways. With Union armies advancing all over Confederate territory and with George McClellan only a few miles from Richmond, death seemed to hover at the door of the nascent Confederacy. Then, in the matter of a few days, things turned upside

Lee banished from the Eastern Theater several generals whose performance displeased him during the Seven Days'—among them, "Prince John" Magruder, who had performed brilliantly on the Peninsula under Johnston but who fell hapless victim to bad luck during the Seven Days' under Lee. Magruder, serving the Trans-Mississippi Theater, would oversee one of the last Confederate surrenders of the war in Galveston, Texas. Here, Magruder (back row, third from left) and Lee (front row, second from left) reunite with several other former generals and dignitaries for a photo. (wc)

down. The Confederates went on the offense. They now had *two* heroes: Jackson in the Valley and Lee outside Richmond. All things seemed possible.

Federals had felt confident of an early victory, but their stinging defeat meant they had to settle down for a bitter struggle that would clearly take all of their determination and resources—and the blood of a generation of young men.

The Seven Days' was also a turning point in American history. McClellan, like many in the Union, was fighting to put the country back together. He did not want to do anything to antagonize the Southern people; he would not condone seizing or destroying their property, and he had no interest in freeing their slaves. His goal was the destruction of the Confederate war machine and nothing more. The people of the South would then be welcomed back into the Union. The Seven Days' campaign was critical in changing that northern view. William A. Blair, in his essay "The Seven Days' and The Radical Persuasion" (from *The Richmond Campaign of 1862*) argues that as McClellan was defeated, so was the moderate Union position. A week earlier, it had seemed that victory was within Union soldiers' grasp, but now they faced a long and costly struggle. Thousands of their young men

Following the Seven Days', Lincoln would begin discussing the very nature of the war with his closest advisers and cabinet. Those conversations would lead to the preliminary Emancipation Proclamation, which Lincoln would write in the summer of 1862. He would finally issue it following the battle of Antietam in September. (loc)

had already been killed or maimed, and the end was nowhere in sight. The more radical members of the government began to argue that a "harder" war would be necessary. Confederate property should be seized or destroyed—anything that supported the rebellion was fair game.

This led, of course, to the question of slavery. At the beginning of the war, many slaves who escaped through Union lines were returned to their masters. The "Radicals" argued that this made no sense. Slaves built the earthworks that protected the enemy; they worked on the farms and in the factories. They freed up more white men to fight for the Confederacy. It was ludicrous to return these valuable assets to the enemy. Rather, they could be used to help the Union army as laborers, teamsters, etc. Some radicals, such as Thaddeus Stevens, argued that the former slaves should even be brought into the army to help fight the Confederates. This would eventually happen— and to effect.

On July 17, 1862, the Militia Act was passed, which stated:

That the President be, and he is hereby, authorized to receive into the service of the United States, for the purpose of constructing intrenchments, or performing camp service or any other labor, or any military or naval service for which they may be found competent, persons of African descent, and such persons shall be enrolled and organized under such regulations, not inconsistent with the Constitution and laws, as the President may prescribe.

Additionally, the Act specified that any male slave of African descent who provided such service, and had been owned by someone who "has levied war or has borne arms against the United States, or adhered to their enemies by giving them aid and comfort," would be forever free. This extended to his mother, wife, and children, provided they also were owned by someone who supported the rebellion.

Armed with this act, Lincoln on July 21 ordered the use of escaped slaves as laborers. On the 22nd, he also took one further step: he discussed his emancipation plan with his cabinet. It was not fully developed, though, and the time was not right to issue it. That would come months later. But the course had changed, and with it the future of the United States. It will never be known when slavery would have expired in America had McClellan defeated Lee and had the war ended then, but the Seven Days' conflict made that question moot; the fate of slavery would be sealed with a Union victory.

The unintended consequences of war can be most ironic. McClellan had sought only to put the Union back together not change the Southern way of life. Lee had successfully turned the Federal army back and had defended the capital. As a result, the Radicals had gained influence in the Federal Government. Now, should the Confederacy lose the war, then the way of life it fought so desperately to protect would perish along with it.

End of the Tour

If you're interested in visiting the Army of the Potomac's base on the James River at Berkeley Plantation—site of Harrison's Landing—turn right as you leave the Malvern Hill parking lot. In 1.1 miles, you will arrive at the junction with modern-day Rt. 5, known as the River Road during the war. Make a left. The plantation is about 11 miles away. You will pass an entrance to Shirley Plantation on the way. Robert E. Lee's mother, Anne Hill Carter, was raised here, and young Robert spent time at the Plantation. Berkeley Plantation is next, and just past that is Westover. All are worth a stop, although the main Westover building is only open at select times during the year.

Otherwise, turn right as you leave the Malvern Hill parking lot. In 1.1 miles, you will arrive at the junction with modern-day Rt. 5. Go right. In 3.5 miles, you will see a sign that mentions the battle of New Market Heights (as mentioned in Chapter Nine). At this time, no land has been saved at this site, so the sign is the only indication of the battle. Rt. 295 is 0.7 miles ahead of you.

If you would like to go to Fort Harrison (also mentioned in Chapter Nine), continue on Rt. 5. You will pass a few signs for Fort Harrison, but it would be best to skip them. In 2.8 miles, you will see a sign for the Richmond National Battlefield site at Fort Harrison on your left. Turn down this road. In about a mile, you will reach Fort Gilmer. A little past this on your left will be the remains of Fort Gregg. A mile farther and you will reach Fort Johnson, on your right. One more half mile and you will reach Fort Harrison.

MAJ·GEN·J.E.B·STUART
COMMANDING·CAVALRY·CORPS
ARMY·NORTHERN·VIRGINIA
CONFEDERATE·STATES·OF·AMERICA
✶ ✶ ✶
THIS·STATUE·ERECTED·BY·HIS·COMRADES
AND·THE·CITY·OF·RICHMOND
A·D·1906

Eyes on the Peninsula: Stuart's Ride around McClellan

APPENDIX A

JUNE 12-15, 1862

BY MARK WILCOX

Early June of 1862 was an important period in the life of the Confederate Army of Northern Virginia, for it was then, on the outskirts of Richmond, that the army would be introduced to a new commander—and this with the Union Army nearly on the doorstep of the capital city.

The first order of business for the newly appointed commanding general, Robert Edward Lee, would be to turn the forces of Maj. Gen. George B. McClellan's Army of the Potomac away from the gates of Richmond. From his headquarters at Dabbs House in Henrico County, Lee would meet with his generals and plan what became known as the Seven Days' Campaign.

Favoring a possible strike on the Federals' right and rear, Lee met with his cavalry commander on June 10 to discuss a reconnaissance in force. He needed information as to the strength of the Union Army there and information on the road network between the Chickahominy and Pamunkey rivers. Commanding the cavalry forces of the Army of Northern Virginia was 29-year-old Brig. Gen. James Ewell Brown "J. E. B." Stuart. A graduate of the United States Military Academy at West Point, class of 1854, Stuart was also a veteran of the old pre-war U.S. Army. Already known in the army for his outlandish style of dress, with his jack boots, lined cape, and cocked hat sporting a peacock's feather, not only did Stuart agree with his commanding general regarding a thrust toward the Federal right, but he came to the meeting with ideas of his own on how it should be accomplished. To reconnoiter the area, Stuart proposed to ride completely around the Union army. General Lee, however, saw no need for such theatrics.

Dedicated in 1907, a statue of J. E. B. Stuart rears up at the intersection of Lombardy Street and Monument Avenue in Richmond. (cm)

On June 11, Stuart received his orders from Lee to scout the rear of the Federal army. Apparently feeling the need to curb young Stuart's excitement in order to keep from endangering his command, Lee added, "You will return as soon as the object of

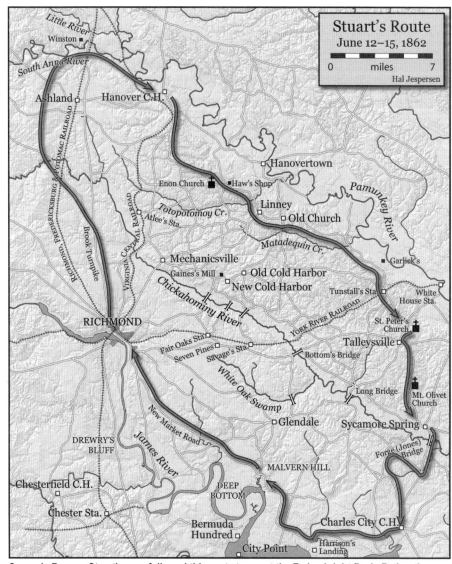

STUART'S ROUTE—Stuart's men followed this route to scout the Federal right flank. Rather than retrace his steps, Stuart determined that the safest and most profitable thing for his troopers to do would be to continue around the enemy. The ride would become the stuff of legend.

your expedition is accomplished, and you must bear constantly in mind, while endeavoring to execute the general purpose of your mission, not to hazard unnecessarily your command or to attempt what your judgment may not approve; but be content to accomplish all the good you can without feeling it necessary to obtain all that might be desired."

Stuart immediately began to put together his reconnaissance force. He selected the 1st and 9th

Virginia Cavalry as well as squadrons from the 4th Virginia and the Mississippi Legion. Altogether, 1,200 Confederate horsemen would make the scout. Accompanying his command was the colonel of the 9th Virginia, Robert E. Lee's own son, Rooney Lee, and nephew, Fitzhugh "Fitz" Lee, colonel of the 1st Virginia. Stuart's chief scout was a young man from Powhatan County, 1st Lt. John Singleton Mosby, who would go on to success of his own as commander of Mosby's Rangers.

At 2 a.m. on June 12, Stuart put his staff into motion with the announcement, "Gentlemen, in ten minutes every man must be in his saddle." By break of day, the troopers had left the Richmond area and were well on their way northwest towards Louisa Courthouse, looking as though their aim were to link up with the army of the indomitable Maj. Gen. Thomas J. "Stonewall" Jackson in the Shenandoah Valley. Eventually, the horsemen turned towards the east and camped near the South Anna River. That first night out, Stuart was nearly captured by Union forces as he slept in a chair at Hickory Hill, the home of Col. Williams Wickham.

On June 13, Mosby scouted the area around Hanover Courthouse; he found it to the rear of the Union Army. As the Southern scouts moved southeast along the road to Old Church, they encountered small numbers of Federal cavalry pickets, proving that McClellan had not extended his lines to the right. For the most part, the gray horsemen easily dispersed these Yankee pickets, although they did take some prisoners.

Commanding a division of U.S. Cavalry was Brig. Gen. Philip St. George Cooke. It was a matter of no little irony that General Cooke happened to be the father-in-law of none other than J.E.B. Stuart himself. Responding to Stuart's activities, Cooke ordered six squadrons of the 5th U.S. Cavalry to reinforce his pickets between Haw's Shop and Totopotomoy Creek, along current Route 606 in Hanover County near Studley, birthplace of Virginia patriot Patrick Henry. But the Rebel cavalry was able to easily scatter these forces, and Stuart was able to cross Totopotomoy Creek.

About a mile south of the creek, at Linney's Grove, Stuart's horsemen encountered a small number of troopers from the 5th U.S. Cavalry

Hickory Hill Plantation in Hanover Country was the home of Lt. Col. Williams Carter Wickham of the 4th Virginia Cavalry, where Robert E. Lee's son Rooney was captured in 1863. (mw)

under the command of Capt. William B. Royal. Stuart ordered his artillery and the 9th Virginia Cavalry to scatter the Federals. Leading the charge of the 9th Virginia was Capt. William Latané. He and the Union commander, Royal, would engage in single combat, both swinging and slashing with sabers. Although Royal was wounded, he succeeded in killing Latané with his pistol before the Federal troopers retired. William Latané would be the only loss suffered by Stuart during the reconnaissance.

Stuart then moved along to the area of Old Church. He encountered another small Union force there, but the Federals fled as soon as they saw the Southerners approach, leaving behind a cache of supplies. Stuart's men grabbed boots, guns, and a quantity of liquor. By this time, Stuart already possessed the information Lee sent him to acquire. He now knew that the Union Army's right flank was only lightly defended, and he had better knowledge of the roads in that area. Now, he had a decision to make.

Stuart had much to consider when deciding how best to get his information back to Lee. Taking a more northerly route, across the Pamunkey, was out of the question as most of the bridges he would need had been destroyed. Retracing his steps to Richmond could be hazardous as the Federals now knew about his presence— going back the way he had come could invite casualties. But crossing the Chickahominy River east of the Union forces, thus riding around McClellan's army might also provide an opportunity for that army to trap him. No matter how Stuart looked at it, there was danger. In the end, he made up his mind: Take the risk and go on. "Tell Fitz Lee to come along," Stuart told a staff member. "I'm going to move on with my column."

At Garlick's Landing on the Pamunkey, in New Kent County, Stuart's forces burned supply wagons and destroyed two schooners. More prisoners were taken. The Confederates attacked Tunstall's Station on the line of the Richmond and York River Railroad, the lead scouts masquerading as the 8th Illinois Cavalry. While there, Rooney Lee's 9th Virginia attempted to ambush a Federal supply train as it was coming into the station, but the train was able to escape the trap. Officers on board later notified the 93rd New York Infantry who were only a mile or so away from Tunstall's. The 93rd immediately began to form a line of battle.

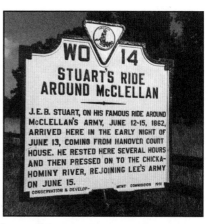

About four miles from Tunstall's was White House Landing on the Pamunkey. Property once owned by George and Martha Washington, the White House was now functioning as McClellan's main supply base. Stuart contemplated destroying the base, which would have forced McClellan to retreat. But ultimately, he felt this risk to his command was too great. He decided to ride on.

This historical marker on state Route 249 in New Kent Country, near Talleysville, commemorates Stuart's Ride. His cavalry passed this way en route to the Chickahominy River crossing. (mw)

By this time Col. Gouverneur Warren, commanding a brigade of the Union V Corps, was behind Stuart. Also, the 1st U.S. Cavalry, with Philip St. George Cooke riding along, and four squadrons of the 6th Pennsylvania Cavalry, were also searching for Stuart. In addition, Brig. Gen. John F. Reynolds and his brigade of Pennsylvania Reserves marched to Tunstall's Station. None of the Federal forces, however, were able to locate Stuart.

By June 14, the Rebel horsemen had been in the saddle for nearly 24 hours. They were exhausted, as was their commander. At one point, Stuart fell asleep in the saddle as his horse continued to walk on. South of New Kent Courthouse, the gray horsemen hoped to cross the Chickahominy River via Jones's Bridge—also known as the Forge Bridge. The river was swollen due to recent rains, and the bridge had been damaged. Unable to cross the river, some of Stuart's officers began to consider the possibility of surrender should a large Union force appear. When asked, Stuart offered another option: "To die game."

Stuart had his men begin repair work on the bridge, knowing that a Federal force could appear at any time. It was tense, but Stuart seemed to take it all in stride, calmly sitting on the riverbank as the work went on. Mosby described Stuart as being in "the gayest humor I ever saw." Within a few hours, the bridge was repaired and the Confederate troopers and their prisoners crossed,

Stuart and his men passed this hotel—which is in Old Church, at the intersection of McClellan and Old Church roads—during their ride. (dc)

leaving the bridge burning behind them. It was still smoldering when a few troopers of the 6th Pennsylvania Cavalry galloped up.

Stuart's force now turned west towards Richmond on the New Market Road, present Route 5. On June 15, Stuart left his command and, along with two men, set out for Richmond. In Charles City County, they stopped in on the Rowland family of Edgewood Plantation for coffee before going on to Richmond. The remainder of Stuart's command joined him in the city the next day.

The reconnaissance was a coup for the Confederate horseman and another feather in the cap for J. E. B. Stuart. General Lee now had the information he desired while Gen. McClellan's Federals, on the other hand, understandably felt some humiliation that Stuart's cavalry force had completely circled their army without capture.

MARK WILCOX is *a park ranger with the National Park Service, Mark Wilcox works at the Richmond Battlefield sites as well as at the Maggie Walker National Historic Site.*

Jeb Stuart's ride would bring his cavalry past Malvern Hill at the start of the Seven Days campaign; Lee would bring his infantry and artillery there at the end of the campaign. (kw)

The Civilians

APPENDIX B

As the war raged through eastern Hanover and Henrico counties, it did not spare the homes of local citizens. Armies marched through their land, crops were destroyed, men were killed in the fields, and the wounded were brought into homes, their blood permanently staining the wood floors. The dead were partially buried in the yards. Some homes, like the Watt house, were seriously damaged by the firing.

At Beaver Dam Creek, the Sydnor families had homes on two adjacent tracts of land. One was "Oakley Hill," situated on Cold Harbor Road; another was "Meadow Farm," just a short distance away. Federal troops occupied both of these farms. William Barrett Sydnor lived on the latter farm with his 16 children, six of whom were in the Confederate Army, including Thomas White Sydnor of the 4th Virginia Cavalry. One son, Henry Clinton Sydnor, later wrote of the Yankee occupation, entitling his tale "A Virginia Boy in the Sixties."

Sydnor told a story about the overseer's wife, who lived on a hill on the plantation; her husband was off in the Confederate Army. Federal officers climbed the hill and taunted her, saying they would soon take Richmond and "capture her husband and send him home to her."

"You have been up on the hill viewing the promised land, have you?" she responded one day. "Well don't you know the prophet Moses climbed the mount and viewed the promised land, but he never got there?"

Dr. William Gaines was one of the most prominent men in the area and a fierce supporter of the Confederate cause. Union troops encamped on his land, Powhite, for about a month. Gaines's daughter, Fanny Gaines Tinsley, kept a diary of her experiences during the war. When the Union troops arrived, she and her mother stayed with their father, who refused to leave the property. She said the Federals "put a guard of thirty men" around their home for protection, with "orders never to let a private enter the yard." One particular guard was posted at the back door for three weeks, and "Mother gave him three meals a day." This did not change her father's opinion at all: legend has

The Watt House, which stands on the Gaines's Mill, is one of the few civilian structures that still remains from the Seven Days'. (cm)

it that if the Federals buried any of their soldiers
on his land, he threatened to dig them up and feed
them to his hogs.

Fighting ravaged the home places of Powhite,
Fairfield, Selwyn, and Puccoon, and the Garthright
house, now part of the Cold Harbor National
Battlefield, also witnessed the action.

Old Cold Harbor's name has puzzled
students of the battle and locals for decades. The
establishment of Isaac Burnett, possibly it earned
the name for offering few amenities, perhaps only
cold food—if it served food at all. A mile or so
to the southwest stood New Cold Harbor Tavern.
Two taverns with nearly the same name became
a source of considerable confusion for the armies
in 1862. Descendants of the owners of New Cold
Harbor state that part of the building standing
in 2016 is the actual tavern. The owner was a
Unionist, surrounded by Confederate neighbors.

The Watt house was known as Springfield at
the time of the battle of Gaines's Mill. Hugh Watt
had passed away in 1854, and his elderly widow,
Sarah, occupied the home. Mrs. Watt, born Sarah
Bohannan Kidd, was born in 1784. She married
Hugh, an Irish immigrant, in 1802. As the battle
became imminent, Mrs. Watt's family had to carry
her from the home and load her into a wagon—
never to return.

The house suffered damage and was used as
a field hospital. During the Great Depression, the
Civilian Conservation Corps made repairs to the
building, which was later restored more fully by
the Richmond National Battlefield Park. Next to

These reenactors depict Richmond civilians enjoying a picnic lunch. The war quickly did away with such niceties. (dc)

the Watt house stands the Adams farm. A silent spectator to the devastating actions of 1862 and 1864, a very historically minded family now owns it. The farm remains private property. Should you visit the battlefield, please respect the family's wishes.

As you travel from the Gaines's Mill battlefield towards Savage's Station, you will pass an old building on your right with a Civil War Trails marker along the roadside. This is the Trent house, headquarters for General McClellan. It is now a private residence. When you reach Wills Church Road on the Glendale battlefield, you might see a portion of an old foundation a few hundred yards to your left. This is all that remains of the Nelson house. That farm suffered the ravages of an intense battle, as did the Whitlock farm and the homes and fields of Richard and Isaac Sykes, all of which are now gone. The Sykes's homes were part of the Gravel Hill area, a community of free African-Americans, which was a rarity at the time.

At Malvern Hill you will see two houses. One, the Crew house, is a reconstruction of the original dwelling, which burned after the war. The other is the West house. This is not an original structure, although at least part of it is built on the wartime foundation. During the battle, the

Sarah Watt was 75 years old in June 1862 and had to be carried from her home as the armies approached. (rnbp)

family hid in the basement and flew a red flag, hoping the Confederates would spare their home from artillery fire. The Malvern house was the original building on the Malvern estate, but it no longer exists, having been destroyed by fire in 1905.

One Confederate veteran remembered the scene at the Malvern house: it was "a century old," and in "a fine state of preservation, and had well withstood the touch of time, up to the time of its desecration and partial ruin by the Lincoln vandals." He remembered draining a small body of water, and therein "a vast amount of amputated limbs were discovered"; he also recalled "a mammoth pit, in which were indiscriminately piled in and covered up, hundreds of Yankee dead."

The owner of the Malvern Hill plantation claimed that his slaves had gone over to the enemy, and he had lost "Fifteen hundred bushels of corn, Twenty one head of cattle, eight mules, thirty head of hogs, ten thousand pounds of blade fodder about eighteen hundred pounds of Bacon," wagons, tools, and even weather boarding and doors from his buildings. Such was the plight of the farmers of Hanover and Henrico counties.

After the armies left in 1862, it would take years before the residents could recover. The suffering was great, and families were in desperate straits. If that were not bad enough, in two years, the armies appeared again to fight major battles on some of the same lands. By that point, Richmond's prewar population of 35,000 had swelled to more than 100,000. The wounded filled homes and factories; space had to be made for prisoners of war. It seemed no home could escape the horrors of warfare.

Sarah Watt, née Sarah Bohannon Kidd (rnbp)

Preservation Efforts

APPENDIX C

In his fascinating "Echoes of 1861-1961," J. Ambler Johnston told the story of early preservation efforts in Richmond: "In the early 1920's, the fields were completely unmarked, overgrown with timber, no roads, no markers, nothing to indicate where the engagements were, and you had to learn to know your way around." He added, "I doubt whether there were more than a dozen people in the city who could have told you where they were located and what battles took place at them."

Around that time, a small group, including Johnston and Douglas Southall Freeman, organized a tour that included veterans from the Old Soldiers Home. The group became extremely enthused and decided that markers had to be put up on the fields, so they raised money among themselves and through the Richmond City Council and placed 62 markers around the battlefields. Today, these are often referred to as "Freeman markers."

To complement the effort, the counties of Hanover and Henrico, where the battles were fought, donated one year of gas tax allowances to the construction of the modern battlefield tour road, Route 156.

In 1927 this group, which called itself the "Richmond Battlefield Parks Corporation," preserved the first battlefield lands. The group donated $18,000 to purchase property in the Fort Harrison area, and they built a log cabin for their headquarters. Other parcels were soon procured or donated at Chickahominy Bluffs, Beaver Dam Creek, Gaines's Mill, Cold Harbor, Drewry's Bluff, and Malvern Hill. Eventually these fields would become part of the National Park Service, and the log cabin would become the first visitor's center.

Standing at the ruins of the Nelson farm, one can see the flagpole of the Glendale National Cemetery in the far treeline. Not too long ago, the land between was under threat of development. Richmond National Battlefield owned only a single acre at Glendale. Thanks to aggressive work by preservation groups in the last decade and a half, hundreds of acres are now protected. (cm)

During the Great Depression, the Civilian Conservation Corps worked at the parks and cleared portions of the land. Over the years, many dignitaries have visited the battlefields, including Ferdinand Foch, David

Sunday visitors drop in at Fort Harrison in the 1930s. The log cabin served as the visitor center and, at one time, as the park's headquarters. (rnbp)

Lloyd George, and Winston Churchill, all of whom were escorted by Dr. Freeman. Contrary to legend, German General Erwin Rommel was not among the visitors.

James Ambler Johnston was a friend of Freeman's and a partner in preservation. He rode on some of the aforementioned excursions and remembered Lloyd George saying, "Well, now before we get to that next turn, let me see if I'm right. Is not such and such a thing what happened just the other side of that turn?"

Before and after images of the Garthright house, initially restored in 1935 and again in 1971 following a 1970 fire. The house sits across from Cold Harbor National Cemetery, adjacent to a Hanover County Civil War park. (rnbp)

RIGHT: **During the depression, the CCC helped to preserve and restore battlefields around Richmond. One location, Fort Hoke, was actually reconstructed.** (rnbp)
BELOW: **CCC sign at Fort Harrison.** (rnbp)

When Field Marshall Foch came to tour the sites, the roads and markers were not yet in place. Johnston said, "For weeks we worked on a map of the Seven Days Campaign with all the names and the legends in French."

Today, the battlefields around Richmond are in the best condition since the war. Although some—notably Seven Pines, Savage's Station, Yellow Tavern, and portions of Cold Harbor—have been lost forever to development, major efforts have been made by preservation organizations to save the land that is available.

On the Gaines's Mill battlefield, great strides have been made over the past 20 years to save precious parcels. In 2011, the Richmond Battlefields Association purchased a few acres on the Confederate side of Boatswain's Swamp (the association has also purchased land at Beaver Dam Creek, Cold Harbor, and other sites). In 2011, the Civil War Trust and the Commonwealth of Virginia teamed up to buy 285 acres of land at Gaines's Mill, and in 2016 the Trust acquired several more acres along the Park road. Before these preservation successes, only 65 acres had been saved at Gaines's Mill. Now, historians and the Park Service can tell a much broader story.

At Glendale, during the 1990s, the Park Service owned but one acre. Thanks to the Civil War Trust (and history-minded land owners), almost the entire battlefield has now been saved, with Park Service interpretation planned to supplement it.

Malvern Hill is another spectacular preservation story. In the early 1990s, the battlefield

Sarah Watt house before restoration (above) and after, in 2016 (top). (rnbp)

was a fragment of what it is today. After successful preservation and restoration efforts, visitors can visit the entire battlefield and have a view that is almost the same as it was in July 1862.

Thanks to the Richmond Battlefields Association and the Civil War Trust, additional parcels of land have been saved at Cold Harbor, and a major tract was saved by the Trust on the Jericho Mill portion of the North Anna battlefield. Land has also been saved at lesser-known battlefields such as First and Second Deep Bottom and Totopotomoy Creek.

Hanover County has also preserved land. A county park at Ox Ford at North Anna preserves part of Lee's "inverted V," and there is a small park located at Cold Harbor, adjacent to part of the Richmond Battlefield Park's Garthright house property.

It has been an amazing period of preservation. Battlefields thought to be lost forever have been saved for present and future generations to visit, enjoy, and learn from.

In 2014, the Civil War Trust turned over 285 preserved acres at Gaines's Mill to the National Park Service. Along with the Richmond Battlefields Association, preservation groups have saved hundreds of acres in the Richmond area. This field is the scene of Longstreet's advance. (dc)

The impact preservation groups have had on the battlefields around Richmond can be seen most dramatically at the adjoining battlefields of Glendale and Malvern Hill. On the following two pages, maps prepared by the Civil War Trust exclusively for Emerging Civil War show how little battlefield land was preserved in 1987 compared to 2017. Over the course of thirty years, preservationists have saved more than 1,600 acres. (Civil War Trust maps by Steven Stanley)

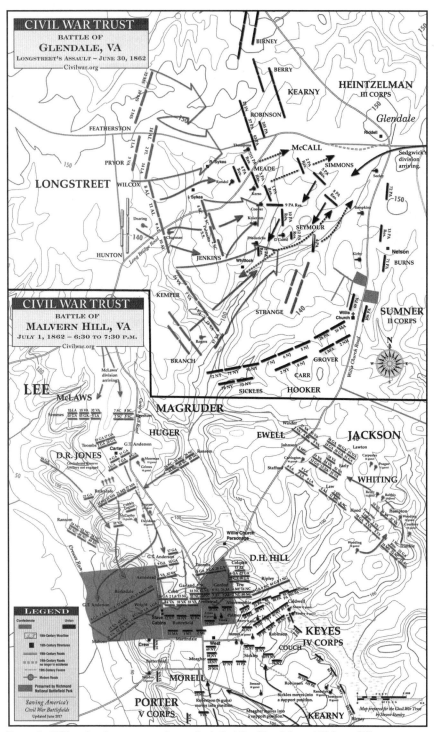

THEN—In 1987, only a few preserved parcels dotted the Glendale and Malvern Hill Battlefields.

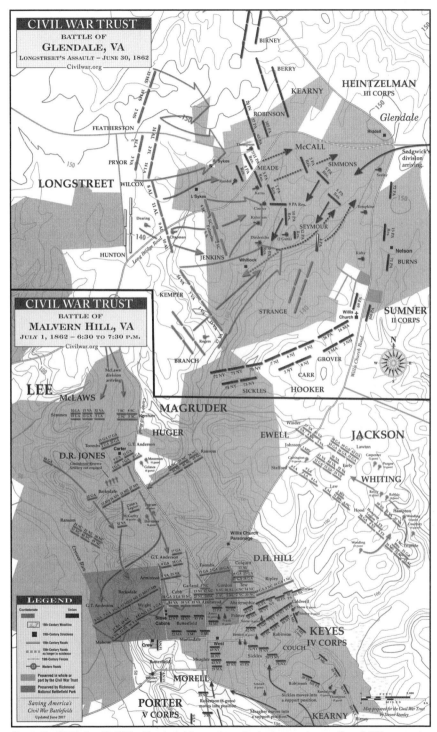

Now—By 2017, the Civil War Trust and its partners had preserved more than 1,600 acres at these battlefields.

THE SEVEN DAYS
JULY 9, 1864

The Army of the Potomac
Maj. Gen. George B. McClellan

SECOND CORPS: Maj. Gen. Edwin V. Sumner
FIRST DIVISION: Brig. Gen. Israel B. Richardson
First Brigade: Brig. Gen. John C. Caldwell
5th New Hampshire • 7th New York • 61st New York • 81st Pennsylvania

Second Brigade: Brig. Gen. Thomas F. Meagher • Col. Robert Nugent
29th Massachusetts • 63rd New York • 60th New York • 88th New York

Third Brigade: Brig. Gen. William H. French
*52nd New York • 57th New York • 64th New York • 66th New York
53rd Pennsylvania • 2nd Delaware*

Division Artillery: Capt. George W. Hazzard
1st New York Light, Battery B • 4th U.S., Batteries A and C

SECOND DIVISION: Brig. Gen. John Sedgwick
First Brigade: Col. Alfred Sully
*15th Massachusetts • 1st Minnesota • 34th New York • 82nd New York
1st Company Massachusetts Sharpshooters • Russell's Sharpshooters*

Second Brigade: Brig. Gen. William W. Burns
69th Pennsylvania • 71st Pennsylvania • 72nd Pennsylvania • 106th Pennsylvania

Third Brigade: Brig. Gen. Napoleon J. T. Dana
19th Massachusetts • 20th Massachusetts • 7th Michigan • 42nd New York

Division Artillery: Col. Charles H. Tomkins
1st Rhode Island Light, Battery A • 1st U.S., Battery I

CORPS RESERVE ARTILLERY RESERVE
1st New York Light, Battery G • 1st Rhode Island Light, Batteries B and G

CORPS CAVALRY
6th New York, companies D, F, H, and K

THIRD CORPS: Brig. Gen. Samuel P. Heintzelman
Second Division: Brig. Gen. Joseph Hooker
First Brigade: Brig. Gen. Cuvier Grover
*1st Massachusetts • 11th Massachusetts • 16th Massachusetts • 2nd New Hampshire
26th Pennsylvania*

Second Brigade: Brig. Gen. Daniel E. Sickles
70th New York • 71st New York • 72nd New York • 73rd New York • 74th New York

Third Brigade: Col. Joseph P. Carr
5th New Jersey • 6th New Jersey • 7th New Jersey • 8th New Jersey • 2nd New York

Division Artillery
1st New York Light, Battery D • 4th New York Light • 1st U.S., Battery H

THIRD DIVISION: Brig. Gen. Philip Kearny
First Brigade: Brig. Gen. John C. Robinson
20th Indiana • 87th New York • 57th Pennsylvania • 63rd Pennsylvania • 105th Pennsylvania

Second Brigade: Brig. Gen. David B. Birney
3rd Maine • 4th Maine • 38th New York • 40th New York • 101st New York

Third Brigade: Brig. Gen. Hiram G. Berry
2nd Michigan • 3rd Michigan • 5th Michigan • 1st New York • 37th New York

Division Artillery
1st Rhode Island, Battery E • 2nd U.S., Battery G

CORPS ARTILLERY RESERVE: Capt. Gustavus DeRussy
6th New York Light • 2nd New Jersey Light • 4th U.S., Battery K

CORPS CAVALRY
3rd Pennsylvania

FOURTH CORPS: Maj. Gen. Erasmus D. Keyes
FIRST DIVISION: Brig. Gen. Darius N. Couch
First Brigade: Brig. Gen. Albion P. Howe
*55th New York • 62nd New York • 93rd Pennsylvania • 98th Pennsylvania
102nd Pennsylvania*

Second Brigade: Brig. Gen. John J. Abercrombie
*65th New York • 67th New York • 23rd Pennsylvania • 31st Pennsylvania
61st Pennsylvania*

Third Brigade: Brig Gen. Innis N. Palmer
7th Massachusetts • 10th Massachusetts • 36th New York • 2nd Rhode Island

Division Artillery
1st Pennsylvania Light, Batteries C and D

SECOND DIVISION: Brig. Gen. John J. Peck
First Brigade: Brig. Gen. Henry M. Naglee
*11th Maine • 56th New York • 100th New York • 52nd Pennsylvania
104th Pennsylvania*

Second Brigade: Brig. Gen. Henry W. Wessells
*81st New York • 85th New York • 92nd New York • 96th New York
98th New York • 85th Pennsylvania • 101st Pennsylvania • 103rd Pennsylvania*

Division Artillery
1st New York Light, Battery H • 7th New York Light

CORPS RESERVE ARTILLERY: Maj. Robert M. West
8th New York Light • 1st Pennsylvania Light, Batteries E and H • 5th U.S., Battery M

CORPS CAVALRY: Col. David M. Gregg
8th Pennsylvania

FIFTH CORPS: Brig. Gen. Fitz John Porter
FIRST DIVISION: Brig. Gen. George W. Morell
First Brigade: Brig. Gen. John H. Martindale
*2nd Maine • 18th Massachusetts (detached) • 22nd Massachusetts • 1st Michigan
13th New York • 25th New York • Massachusetts Sharpshooters (2nd Company)*

Second Brigade: Brig. Gen. Charles Griffin
9th Massachusetts • 4th Michigan • 14th New York • 62nd Pennsylvania

Third Brigade: Brig. Gen. Daniel Butterfield
12th New York • 17th New York (detached) • 44th New York • 16th Michigan
83rd Pennsylvania • Michigan Sharpshooters (Brady's Company)

Division Artillery: Capt. William B. Weeden
Massachusetts Light, Batteries C and E • 1st Rhode Island Light, Battery C
5th U.S., Battery D

Division Sharpshooters: Col. Hiram Berdan
1st U.S. Sharpshooters

SECOND DIVISION: Brig. Gen. George Sykes
First Brigade: Col. Robert C. Buchanan
3rd U.S. • 4th U.S. • 12th U.S. • 14th U.S.

Second Brigade: Maj. Charles S. Lovell
2nd U.S. • 6th U.S. • 10th U.S. • 11th U.S. • 17th U.S.

Third Brigade: Col. Gouverneur K. Warren
5th New York • 10th New York

Division Artillery: Capt. Stephen H. Weed
3rd U.S., Batteries L and M • 5th U.S., Battery I

THIRD DIVISION: Brig. Gen. George A. McCall; Brig. Gen. Truman
Seymour
First Brigade: Brig. Gen. John F. Reynolds; Col. Seneca G. Simmons; Col.
C. Biddle Roberts
1st Pennsylvania Reserves • 2nd Pennsylvania Reserves • 5th Pennsylvania Reserves
8th Pennsylvania Reserves • 13th Pennsylvania Reserves

Second Brigade: Brig. Gen. George G. Meade
3rd Pennsylvania Reserves • 4th Pennsylvania Reserves • 7th Pennsylvania Reserves
11th Pennsylvania Reserves

Third Brigade: Brig. Gen. Truman Seymour; Col. C. Feger Jackson
6th Pennsylvania Reserves (detached) • 9th Pennsylvania Reserves
10th Pennsylvania Reserves • 12th Pennsylvania Reserves

Division Artillery:
1st Pennsylvania Light, Batteries A, B, and G • 5th U.S., Battery C

Division Cavalry
4th Pennsylvania

Corps Cavalry
8th Illinois

Artillery Reserve: Col. Henry J. Hunt
First Brigade: Lt. Col. William Hays
2nd U.S., Batteries A, B, L, and M • 3rd U.S., Batteries C and G
Second Brigade: Lt. Col. George W. Getty
1st U.S., Batteries E, G, and K • 4th U.S, Battery G • 5th U.S., Batteries A and K

Third Brigade: Maj. Albert Arndt
1st Battalion • New York Light, Batteries A, B, C, and D

Fourth Brigade: Maj. E. R. Petherbridge
Maryland Light, Batteries A and B

Fifth Brigade: Capt. J. Howard Carlisle
2nd U.S., Battery E • 3rd U.S., Batteries F and K

Siege Train
1st Connecticut Heavy

SIXTH CORPS: Brig. Gen. William B. Franklin
First Division: Brig. Gen. Henry W. Slocum
First Brigade: Brig. Gen. George W. Taylor
1st New Jersey • 2nd New Jersey • 3rd New Jersey • 4th New Jersey

Second Brigade: Brig. Gen. Joseph J. Bartlett
5th Maine • 16th New York • 27th New York • 96th Pennsylvania

Third Brigade: Brig. Gen. John Newton
18th New York • 31st New York • 32nd New York • 95th Pennsylvania

Division Artillery
Massachusetts Light, Battery A • 1st New Jersey Light • 2nd U.S., Battery D

Second Division: Brig. Gen. William F. Smith
First Brigade: Brig. Gen. Winfield S. Hancock
6th Maine • 43rd New York • 49th Pennsylvania • 5th Wisconsin

Second Brigade: Brig. Gen. William T. H. Brooks
2nd Vermont • 3rd Vermont • 4th Vermont • 5th Vermont • 6th Vermont

Third Brigade: Brig. Gen. John W. Davidson
7th Maine • 20th New York • 33rd New York • 49th New York • 77th New York

Division Artillery
1st New York Light, Battery E • 1st New York Independent Light • 3rd New York Independent Light • 5th U.S., Battery F

Division Cavalry
5th Pennsylvania, Companies I and K

UNATTACHED CAVALRY
1st New York

ARMY CAVALRY RESERVE: Brig. Gen. Philip St. George Cooke
*6th Pennsylvania • 1st U.S., Companies A, C, F, and H
5th U.S., Companies A, D, F, H, and I • 6th U.S.*

VOLUNTEER ENGINEERS: Brig. Gen. Daniel P. Woodbury
15th New York Engineers • 50th New York Engineers • Battalion U.S. Engineers

AT WHITE HOUSE: (on Pamunkey) Brig. Gen. Silas Casey
*11th Pennsylvania Cavalry, Companies B, D, E, I, and K • 1st New York Light, Battery F
93rd New York, Companies B, C, D, E, G, and I*

AT MCCLELLAN'S HEADQUARTERS
*McClellan's Dragoons • Sturges's Rifles • 93rd New York Infantry, Companies A, F, H, and K • 8th U.S. Infantry, Companies F and G • Oneida, New York Cavalry
2nd U.S. Cavalry • 4th U.S. Cavalry, Companies A and E*

* * *

The Army of Northern Virginia
Gen. Robert E. Lee

JACKSON'S COMMAND: Maj. Gen. Thomas J. Jackson
WHITING'S DIVISION: Brig. Gen. William Whiting
Hood's Brigade: Brig. Gen. John B. Hood
1st Texas • 4th Texas • 5th Texas • 18th Georgia • Hampton's Legion

Law's Brigade: Col. Evander Law
4th Alabama • *2nd Mississippi* • *11th Mississippi* • *6th North Carolina*

Jackson's Division
Winder's Brigade: Brig. Gen. Charles S. Winder
2nd Virginia • *4th Virginia* • *5th Virginia* • *27th Virginia* • *33rd Virginia*
Allegheny Battery • *Rockbridge Artillery*

Jones's Brigade: Lt. Col. R.H. Cunningham, Jr.; Brig. Gen. John R. Jones
21st Virginia • *42nd Virginia* • *48th Virginia* • *1st Virginia Battalion*
Richmond Hampden Artillery Battery

Fulkerson's Brigade: Col. E. V. Fulkerson; Col. E. T. H. Warren; Brig.
Gen. Wade Hampton
10th Virginia • *23rd Virginia* • *37th Virginia* • *Danville Artillery Battery*

Lawton's Brigade: Brig. Gen. Alexander R. Lawton
13th Georgia • *26th Georgia* • *31st Georgia* • *38th Georgia*
60th Georgia (4th Battalion) • *61st Georgia*

Unattached Artillery
Jackson Battery

Ewell's Division: Maj. Gen. Richard Ewell
Elzey's Brigade: Brig. Gen. Arnold Elzey; Col. James A. Walker;
Brig. Gen. Jubal A. Early
12th Georgia • *13th Virginia* • *25th Virginia* • *31st Virginia* • *44th Virginia*
52nd Virginia • *58th Virginia*

Trimble's Brigade: Brig. Gen. Isaac R. Trimble
15th Alabama • *21st Georgia* • *16th Mississippi* • *21st North Carolina*
1st North Carolina Battalion • *Henrico Artillery Battery*

Taylor's Brigade: Brig. Gen. Richard Taylor; Col. I. G. Seymour; Col.
Leroy A. Stafford
6th Louisiana • *7th Louisiana* • *8th Louisiana* • *9th Louisiana*
1st Louisiana Special Battalion • *Charlottesville Artillery Battery*

Maryland Line: Col. Bradley T. Johnson
1st Maryland • *Baltimore Artillery Battery*

HILL'S DIVISION: Maj. Gen. Daniel H. Hill
Rodes's Brigade: Brig. Gen. Robert E. Rodes
3rd Alabama • 5th Alabama • 6th Alabama • 12th Alabama • 26th Alabama

G. B. Anderson's Brigade: Brig. Gen. George B. Anderson
2nd North Carolina • 4th North Carolina • 14th North Carolina • 30th North Carolina

Garland's Brigade: Brig. Gen. Samuel Garland, Jr.
*5th North Carolina • 12th North Carolina • 13th North Carolina
20th North Carolina • 23rd North Carolina*

Colquitt's Brigade: Col. Alfred H. Colquitt
13th Alabama • 6th Georgia • 23rd Georgia • 27th Georgia • 28th Georgia

Ripley's Brigade: Brig. Gen. Roswell S. Ripley
44th Georgia • 48th Georgia • 1st North Carolina • 3rd North Carolina

Division Artillery
*Jeff Davis Battery • King William Battery • Long Island (Virginia) Battery (temporarily attached)
Hardaway's Battery • Richmond Orange Battery • Rhett's Battery • Hanover Battery*

MAGRUDER'S COMMAND: Maj. Gen. John B. Magruder
JONES'S DIVISION: Brig. Gen. David R. Jones
Toombs's Brigade: Brig. Gen. Robert Toombs
2nd Georgia • 15th Georgia • 17th Georgia • 20th Georgia

G. T. Anderson's Brigade: Col. George T. Anderson
1st Georgia • 7th Georgia • 8th Georgia • 9th Georgia • 11th Georgia

Division Artillery
*Wise Battery • Washington Battery • Sumter Battery, Company E • Madison Battery
Ashland Battery • Capt. W. J. Dabney's Battery*

McLAWS'S DIVISION: Maj. Gen. Lafayette McLaws
Semmes's Brigade: Brig. Gen. Paul J. Semmes
*10th Georgia • 53rd Georgia • 5th Louisiana • 10th Louisiana • 15th Virginia
32nd Virginia • Manly's Battery*

Kershaw's Brigade: Brig. Gen. Joseph B. Kershaw
*2nd South Carolina • 3rd South Carolina • 7th South Carolina • 8th South Carolina
Alexandria Battery*

Cobb's Brigade: Brig. Gen. Howell Cobb
*16th Georgia • 24th Georgia • Cobb's Legion • 2nd Louisiana
15th North Carolina • Troup Battery*

Griffith's Brigade: Brig. Gen. Richard Griffith; Col. William Barksdale
*13th Mississippi • 17th Mississippi • 18th Mississippi • 21st Mississippi
Richmond Howitzers, 1st Company*

Division Artillery: Col. Stephen D. Lee
Amherst Battery • Magruder Battery • Pulaski Battery • James City Battery

LONGSTREET'S DIVISION: Maj. Gen. James Longstreet
Kemper's Brigade: Brig. Gen. James L. Kemper
*1st Virginia • 7th Virginia • 11th Virginia • 17th Virginia • 24th Virginia
Loudon Battery*

R. H. Anderson's Brigade: Brig. Gen. Richard H. Anderson
*2nd South Carolina Rifles • 4th South Carolina • 5th South Carolina
6th South Carolina • Palmetto Sharpshooters*

Pickett's Brigade: Brig. Gen. George E. Pickett; Col. Eppa Hunton; Col.
John B. Strange
8th Virginia • 18th Virginia • 19th Virginia • 28th Virginia • 56th Virginia

Wilcox's Brigade: Brig. Gen. Cadmus M. Wilcox
8th Alabama • 9th Alabama • 10th Alabama • 11th Alabama • Thomas Battery

Pryor's Brigade: Brig. Gen. Roger A. Pryor
*14th Alabama • 2nd Florida • 14th Louisiana • 1st Louisiana Battalion
3rd Virginia • Donaldsville Battery*

Featherston's Brigade: Brig. Gen. Winfield S. Featherston
*12th Mississippi • 19th Mississippi • 2nd Mississippi Battalion
Richmond Howitzers (3rd Company)*

Division Artillery
Washington Artillery 1st, 2nd, 3rd, and 4th Companies • Lynchburg Battery • Dixie Battery

HUGER'S DIVISION: Maj. Gen. Benjamin Huger
Mahone's Brigade: Brig. Gen. William Mahone
*6th Virginia • 12th Virginia • 16th Virginia • 41st Virginia • 49th Virginia
Portsmouth Battery • Lynchburg Beauregard Battery*

Wright's Brigade: Brig. Gen. Ambrose R. Wright
44th Alabama • *3rd Georgia* • *4th Georgia* • *22nd Georgia* • *1st Louisiana*
Virginia Light Artillery, Company D • *Sumter Artillery, Company A*

Armistead's Brigade: Brig. Gen. Lewis A. Armistead
9th Virginia • *14th Virginia* • *38th Virginia* • *53rd Virginia* • *57th Virginia*
5th Virginia Battalion • *Fauquier Battery* • *Goochland Battery*

HILL'S LIGHT DIVISION: Maj. Gen. Ambrose P. Hill
Field's Brigade: Brig. Gen. Charles W. Field
40th Virginia • *47th Virginia* • *55th Virginia* • *60th Virginia*

Gregg's Brigade: Brig. Gen. Maxcy Gregg
1st South Carolina • *1st South Carolina Rifles* • *12th South Carolina*
13th South Carolina • *14th South Carolina*

J. R. Anderson's Brigade: Brig. Gen. Joseph R. Anderson; Col. Edward L. Thomas
14th Georgia • *35th Georgia* • *45th Georgia* • *49th Georgia* • *3rd Louisiana Battalion*

Branch's Brigade: Brig. Gen. Lawrence O. Branch
7th North Carolina • *18th North Carolina* • *28th North Carolina*
33rd North Carolina • *37th North Carolina*

Archer's Brigade: Brig. Gen. James J. Archer
5th Alabama Battalion • *19th Georgia* • *1st Tennessee* • *7th Tennessee* • *14th Tennessee*

Pender's Brigade: Brig. Gen. William D. Pender
2nd Arkansas Battalion • *16th North Carolina* • *22nd North Carolina*
34th North Carolina • *38th North Carolina* • *22nd Virginia Battalion*

Division Artillery: Lt. Col. Lewis M. Coleman
1st Maryland Battery • *Charleston German Battery* • *Fredericksburg Battery*
Crenshaw's Battery • *Letcher's Battery* • *Johnson's Battery* • *Masters's Battery*
Pee Dee Battery • *Purcell Battery*

DEPARTMENT OF NORTH CAROLINA: Maj. Gen. Theophilus H. Holmes
Ransom's Brigade: Brig. Gen. Robert Ransom, Jr.
24th North Carolina • *25th North Carolina* • *26th North Carolina*
35th North Carolina • *48th North Carolina* • *49th North Carolina*

Daniel's Brigade: Brig. Gen. Junius Daniel
43rd North Carolina • 45th North Carolina • 50th North Carolina
Burroughs Cavalry Battalion

Walker's Brigade: Brig. Gen. John G. Walker; Col. Van H. Manning
3rd Arkansas • 2nd Georgia Battalion • 27th North Carolina • 46th North Carolina
30th Virginia

Division Artillery
Branch's Battery • Brem's Battery • Capt. Thomas French's Battery
Graham's Battery • Grandy's Battery • Lloyd's Battery

Wise's Command: Brig. Gen. Henry A. Wise
26th Virginia • 46th Virginia • 10th Virginia Cavalry (with Stuart)
Andrews' Battery • Capt. A. D. Armistead's Battery • Capt. D. A. French's Battery
Nelson Battery

Reserve Artillery: Brig. Gen. William N. Pendleton
1st Virginia: Col. J. Thomas Brown
Williamsburg Battery • Richmond Fayette Battery • Richmond Howitzers

Jones's Battalion: Maj. H. P. Jones
Long Island Artillery • Orange Richmond Artillery • Rhett's South Carolina Battery

Nelson's Battalion: Maj. William Nelson
Fluvanna Battery • Amherst Battery • Morris Battery

Richardson's Battalion: Maj. Charles Richardson
Fluvanna Battery • Milledge's Battery • Ashland Battery

Sumter (Georgia) Battalion: Lt. Col. A. S. Cutts
Hamilton's Battery, Companies A, B, D, and E

Cavalry: Brig. Gen. J. E. B. Stuart
1st North Carolina • 1st Virginia • 2nd Virginia • 3rd Virginia • 4th Virginia
5th Virginia • 9th Virginia • 10th Virginia • Critcher's Battalion • Cobb's Legion
Hampton Legion • Jeff Davis Legion • Stuart Horse Artillery • Chew's Battery

Suggested Reading

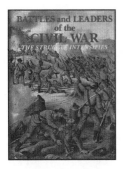

Battles and Leaders of the Civil War, Vol. 2
Castle Book Sales
ISBN: 0-89009-570-1

Selected first-hand accounts by Union and
Confederate commanders such as Fitz John Porter,
William B. Franklin, Daniel Harvey Hill, James
Longstreet, and others. An interesting read, but a
critical eye is recommended.

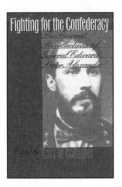

Fighting for the Confederacy
Edited by Gary W. Gallagher
University of North Carolina Press, 1989
ISBN: 978-0-8078-4722-0
An interesting and highly readable first-hand
account. Very well balanced and fair. Alexander
also wrote *Military Memoirs of a Confederate*. Both
books deal with the entire war, but provide useful
information on the Seven Days'.

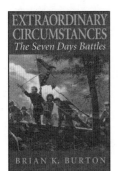

Extraordinary Circumstances: The Seven Days Battles
Brian Burton
Indiana University Press, 2001
ISBN: 978-0-253-33963-8

A detailed, well-written account of the Seven
Days. A must-read for anyone seeking more in-
depth knowledge of the campaign.

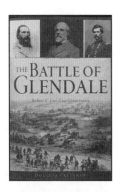

The Battle of Glendale: Robert E. Lee's Lost Opportunity
Douglas Crenshaw
Arcadia Publishing, 2017
ISBN: 978-1-62619-892-0

An account of the battle at Glendale, where Lee missed his best chance to inflict a devastating blow on McClellan's army.

Lee's Lieutenants (Vol. 1)
Douglas Southall Freeman
Charles Scribner's Sons, 1942
ISBN: 0-684-15486-2

Freeman's follow-up the R. E. Lee biography studies Lee's interactions with his commanders.

The Richmond Campaign of 1862: The Peninsula & the Seven Days
Edited by Gary W. Gallagher
The University of North Carolina Press, 2000
ISBN: 978-0-8078-2552-5

A collection of essays by leading historians. Provides outstanding insight on topics such as Jackson's role in the campaign, the travails of John Bankhead Magruder, the attack at Gaines's Mill, Malvern Hill and others. A most interesting and informative read.

Henrico County Field of Honor
Louis H. Manarin
Published by Henrico County, Virginia

A two-volume set about the battles in Henrico
County. Full of interesting information, good
maps, well written. Available from the Henrico
County, Virginia, Department of Parks &
Recreation.

To The Gates of Richmond: The Peninsula Campaign
Stephen W. Sears
Ticknor & Fields, 1992
ISBN: 0-89919-790-6

A highly readable account of the Peninsula
Campaign and Seven Days'. Solidly researched
and highly recommended. A must-read.

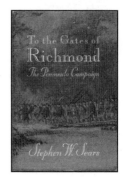

About the Author

Doug Crenshaw is a volunteer for the Richmond National Battlefield Park and a member of the Richmond Civil War Roundtable. He speaks, presents, and leads tours of the battle. His book, *Fort Harrison and The Battle of Chaffin's Farm*, was nominated in the nonfiction category for a Library of Virginia Literary award. He has also written *The Battle of Glendale: Robert E. Lee's Lost Opportunity*. By day, he is a strategic IT sourcing manager who has studied history at Randolph-Macon College and the University of Richmond.

Doug is a descendant of the Sydnor family that lived at Beaver Dam Creek during that battle and the Binford family that lived behind the Malvern Hill battlefield.

Doug is author of a companion volume to this book, also part of the Emerging Civil War Series, that focuses on the 1862 Peninsula Campaign that preceded the Seven Days.